Encyclopedia of
Medicinal Herbs

Encyclopedia of Medicinal HERBS

with the
Herb-O-Matic Locator Index

Former title: *Modern Encyclopedia of Herbs*

JOSEPH M. KADANS, N.D., Ph.D.

AN
ARCO
BOOK

ARCO PUBLISHING COMPANY, INC.
219 Park Avenue South, New York, N.Y. 10003

Published by ARCO PUBLISHING COMPANY, INC.
219 Park Avenue South, New York, N.Y. 10003
by arrangement with Parker Publishing Company, Inc.

Third Printing, 1975

Library of Congress Catalog Number 79-158469
ISBN 0-668-02487-9

Printed in the United States of America

INTRODUCTION

Herbs were recorded in use as early as 2500 B.C. Ancient clay tablets found revealed that the ancient Sumerians used them. Also, the ancient Assyrians knew about the virtues of approximately 250 herbs. The ancient Egyptians, as early as 1600 B.C., used elderberry, pomegranate bark, wild lettuce, wormwood, hemlock and other herbs for health. The Greeks of old used herbs such as mustard, cinnamon, gentian, rhubarb and many others. A pupil of Aristotle wrote ten books on the history of plants and Alexander the Great made a number of expeditions into Africa, Persia and India and brought back herbs in use in those countries.

A Roman soldier and writer, Pliny, the Elder, wrote 47 large volumes on natural history, containing information about 1000 plants.

Ancient physicians and philosophers used the herbs to cure the sick. A German botanist, Otto Brunfels, as early as 1530 published three volumes with woodcuts of 229 plants, which was the first publication of good botanical illustrations. A Portuguese scientist, Garcia da Orta, in 1573, wrote a valuable treatise on the herbs of India.

Carl Von Linne, a Swedish botanist, published material on botany in 1737. The study of herbs was stated to be the mother of all scientific discipline by Professor M. J. Schleiden of Jena in 1842.

The standing of herbology as a science in the United States has been slow to develop but since the turn of the 20th century has grown by leaps and bounds. It is called by various names other than herbology, such as materia medica, botany, pharmacology, vegetable drugs, or pharmacognosy.

Herbs and spices. A dictionary defines an herb as a seed plant which does not develop woody persistent tissue, as that of a shrub or a tree, but is more or less soft or succulent. A spice is any of the various vegetable productions which are fragrant or aromatic and pungent to the taste. Thus herbs may be spices as well as herbs.

Most herbs and spices are dried or cured under the sun of the countries in which they grow and are cultivated. For example, the ginger root is dug from the earth and then is cleaned before it is dried and exported. Sometimes it is also peeled and sometimes some ginger root is boiled in sugar and preserved before it reaches the consumer. Cloves are flower buds while peppercorns are dried berries. The nutmeg is the dried seed of the kernel of the fruit of a tropical tree.

Herbs as medicines. The very first and only true medicines ever used were those derived from the vegetable kingdom. Any vegetables appearing on the table are considered as foods, while any bitter tasting vegetable or growth is considered as a medicine. It is almost forgotten that in the olden days bitters were common to the table. They were made from herbs that had ample supplies of potash present and were very good tonics because they contained potassium, a mineral that is the building cement of muscle and nerve tissue. Animals, such as horses, often know what foods are good for them. Horses will often eat fence rails because the wood is filled to a degree with potash, containing potassium.

Herbs as healing agents. Herbs act as astringents, alkalinizers, acidifiers, tonics, diuretics, diaphoretics, laxatives and serve other purposes.

There is a class of herbs known as nervines, which are nerve foods. These herbs are mineral foods furnishing potash, magnesium and phosphorus. The nerves themselves are made up of potassium, magnesium, phosphorus and sodium in a major degree, although there are other elements. Lecithin is also a major organic element and therefore the presence of lecithin in the food is essential for the nerves to be regulated and relaxed.

Grains have an embryo in their centers and it is in the embryo that lecithin, Vitamin E and phosphorus are found. This is why whole grain cereals are so much better for us. Even better yet is the sprout, for when the seed starts to open and come to life, then the activity of life is increased and the values are more easily assimilated into the body. Lecithin is in the oil of the grain and is more or less destroyed by heating, due to the oxidation of the phosphorus. Therefore, the raw sprouts are excellent foods.

Nervines. There are two classes of nerve foods. There are the excitors and the relaxors or depressors. The excitors are the highly acid factors and low in mineral content. The depressors are the elements that conserve or restrict the flow of energy and are more alkaline. Bromine is one of the depressors. Other depressors are any inorganic substances high in carbon and low in hydrogen. Alcohol slowly starves the tissues and more especially the nerves. Alcohol relaxes the nerves, for the minerals are taken from the nerves by the alcoholic action, and may also cause the tissues to become subject to malnutrition and slow starvation.

Organic foods and nerves. Organic foods such as celery, cucumbers, garlic, honey, molasses, red pepper, ginger, and cloves have a direct effect on the nerves and tend to assist in maintaining a reserve of energy. Therefore they are sources of nerve regeneration as well as providing minerals. Iodine compounds in foods, especially in ocean foods, have a direct action through the thyroid gland, to stimulate the cells and tissues and excite the nerves to contraction. This contraction is brought about by the action of iodine itself. Ocean plants furnish iodine in the best form. Health food stores have dulse and kelp, and these are best in all respects for slow assimilation, along with other minerals that are common to the ocean plants that furnish potassium with iodine. Ocean plants or herbs are a fine source of minerals for health.

THE NAMING OF PLANTS AND HERBS

CARL LINNE: Also known as Carl Linnaeus, Linne was born in Sweden in 1707. He wrote numerous botanical books and became an outstanding authority in the three kingdoms of nature

—plants, animals and minerals. He became a university professor at Upsala, Sweden and he had a great influence on students.

Binomial nomenclature: The system of binomial nomenclature began with his writing on the system known as "Linnaeus in Species Plantarum" in 1753. Linne gave the plants two names, one representing the genus or family group, just as "Johnson" is a family name and the other name representing the species. The system founded by Linne so many years ago is in daily use today, when plants number in the hundreds of thousands.

Sexuality in plants: Linne decided upon the plan of using stamens and pistils as a basis for his classification. He located thirteen classes, based on the number of stamens, from 1 to 11, then 20 stamens, then larger numbers. There are two classes based on the relative lengths of stamens; four classes dealing with connected stamens; one class in which stamens and pistils are consolidated; three classes with imperfect flowers; and one class without stamens or pistils, the cryptogams; for a total of 24 classes. The classes are further divided into orders, pertaining to the number of pistils.

Definitions of stamens and pistils: The stamen is the pollen-bearing floral organ of a flower. The stamen has two parts, the slender stalk (filament) and a double-celled sac (anther) containing the pollen. The pollen is the essential or main part of the stamen.

The pistil normally occupies the center of the flower and consists of the ovary and the stigma. Ovules develop within the ovary in a closed sac. An ovule is a body within the ovary which, upon being fertilized, becomes a seed. Another word for the ovule is ovum or small unfertilized egg. The fertilized ovum becomes an embryo and when the development is complete becomes a seed. There is an opening in the pistil through which the pollen enters to fecundate the ovum.

Terminology: The three categories of the forms of life established by Linne are genera, species and varieties. For example, the genus of the pome fruits is Pyrus. The species of the apple is called Malus. The variety of the apple is Paradisiaca. In writing, therefore, the botanical name of the apple is Pyrul Malus.

To refer to the variety, the full botanical name is Pyrul Malus var. paradisiaca, or the paradise apple.

In looking at a botanical name, therefore, the first word of the name is the genus, the second word is the species and the third is usually the variety.

Species: A definition of a species is a kind of plant or animal that is distinct from other kinds in marked or essential features, with good characteristics of identification. Also, it may be assumed that there will be a continuing succession of the species from generation to generation.

SCOPE OF THIS ENCYCLOPEDIA

This Encyclopedia lists herbs alphabetically by their more popularly known names. Their botanical names are included as well. Very often herbs are also known by several other popularly known names, and these names are included for a complete cross reference under each listed herb.

Each herb's effects and reported usage are listed for reference purposes only. The Herb-O-Matic Locator Index will be found to be exceedingly helpful in locating the names of herbs of value for various ailments.

A section on herbs and spices used in cookery is included as the last part of the book.

JOSEPH M. KADANS, N.D., PH.D.

Encyclopedia of
Medicinal Herbs

ABSCESS ROOT

Also known as American Greek
Valerian, False Jacob's Ladder,
Sweatrcot.

Botanical name: Polemonium reptans.

Effects and reported uses: This herb has a stimulating
effect upon various glands so as to produce considerable
perspiration. It has been recommended for various lung diseases, coughs, colds and bronchial disturbances, especially
where there is high fever. The recommended dosage is to
place one ounce of the herb into a pint of boiling water
and to allow the solution to cool to a temperature suitable
for drinking. The solution may be taken in quantities of one-
half cup at a time two or three times a day.

ACACIA

Also known as Gum Arabic,
Egyptian Thorn, Gum Acacia,
Tamarisk, Catechu.

Botanical names: Acacia Senegal, acacia Arabica, acacia vera, acacia decurrens.

Habitat: Northern Africa, Egypt and Middle-east countries.

Growth needs: A hardy plant that needs little water. Requires considerable sunshine for growth. It is an abundant desert bush.

Description: This is a small tree or shrub but has been known to reach a height of 40 feet. The bark of the tree yields a gum that flows naturally as a thick and frothy liquid which turns into small tear-like globules. The bark of the acacia tree contains a large quantity of tannin.

Part used: Mainly the exudate (moisture) of the bark.

Effects: The gum has a soothing or softening effect upon the skin or mucous membrane to which it is applied. It also has an astringent effect, contracting and hardening tissues so as to limit secretion of glands. Acacia is also said to have nutritive qualities, nourishing tissues to which it is applied.

Recorded uses: A number of authorities have noted the following conditions for which acacia has been found to be of value:

BURNS: By reason of a high tannic acid content, widely known for use in treatment of burns, acacia may be applied to burned areas, having a soothing effect, preventing air from contacting the burn, nourishing the tissue and preventing blistering.

ULCERS: The astringent effect, causing contraction of tissues and tending to arrest discharges, makes acacia valuable for ulcerated areas, such as ulcers of the mouth and gums or other areas.

LOOSE TEETH: When placed into boiling water, acacia becomes an adhesive mucilage and the combination of the contracting tissue effect and the mucilage effect tends to fasten loose teeth.

DIARRHEA: When loose bowels are the result of inflammation of the mucous membrane of the intestines, this is often accompanied by ulcerations of the intestines, fever and bloody evacuations, a condition known as dysentery. In addition to a liquid diet and rest in bed, the drinking of liquids containing a small amount of acacia reportedly aids in the healing processes within the intestines. This should probably be combined with the use of enemas containing a solution of acacia for direct cleansing of the intestinal tract.

COUGHS: An authority on herbs states that acacia is used as an ingredient in medicinal compounds for the treatment of coughs and for hoarseness in the throat. The herb is valuable in this connection because of its soothing effect upon the mucous membranes.

FEVER: While fever is a symptom rather than a disease, acacia, because of its soothing effect upon tissue, has the effect of bringing about a reduction in excessive body temperature, according to one of the herbal authorities.

ACONITE

**Also known as Monkshood,
Wolfsbane, Cuckoo's Cap, Blue
Rocket, Friar's Cap, Jacob's
Chariot.**

Botanical name: Aconitum Napellus.

Effects and reported uses: Made from the dried tuberous
root of this herb plant, the effect is that of a sedative or de-
pressant. It has been used successfully to reduce pain and
fever and consequently has been widely used in combating
scarlet fever, inflammation of the stomach (gastritis), nerve
pains of the face (facial neuralgia), inflammation of the
mucous membrane (catarrh), ulcerated tonsils, croup and
heart palpitation and spasm. Only a small amount is required for effect, such as one or two drops of a fluid extract
of the root in a cup of warm water.

Special warning: There are a few herbs which, when
taken in excess, can be very dangerous and even fatal. Aco-
nite is one of these herbs. An excessive amount may be too
depressive for the heart to continue operating. If taken in
excess, vomiting should be induced.

ACORN

**This is the well-known fruit of
the Oak tree.**

Botanical name: Quercus robur.

Effects and reported uses: The acorn, when ground into
powder and mixed with water, tends to contract and harden

tissues and to limit secretion action by the glands. This astringent action has made the mixture applicable for treatment of diarrhea.

ADDER'S TONGUE

Also known as Serpent's Tongue, Dog's Tooth Violet, Yellow Snowdrop, Rattlesnake Violet, Yellow Snakeleaf.

Botanical names: The American Adder's Tongue is known as Erythronium Americanum and the English Adder's Tongue is known as Ophioglossum vulgatum.

Habitat: United States. It will also grow in other temperate zones.

Growth needs: Rich earth. Grows readily in sunshine with or without shade.

Description: This plant is of the lily family, with two pear-shaped pale green leaves and a single drooping yellow flower.

Parts used: The underground bulb, from which the plant grows, and the leaves.

Effects: When swallowed, it will cause vomiting and so is an emetic. When placed directly upon tissue, it has a soothing and softening effect and so it is also an emollient.

Recorded uses: The fresh leaves may be used whole but preferably should be somewhat bruised and applied directly to ulcers or tumors. In addition, the "tea" resulting from pouring some boiling water over the leaves and allowing it to stand until tolerable for drinking may be taken several times a day for absorption into the body. Another method is to extract the juice from the plant and mix into boiling water, one teaspoon to a cup of water. This herb is reputed to be valuable in treating tuberculosis involving diseased glands and also for scurvy, the disease caused by a deficiency of Vitamin C and marked by weakness, anemia and bleeding from the mucous membrane or the skin. Another use for this herb is the relief it often affords in cases of hiccups and in conditions of swelling due to accumulation of fluid in various body cavities known as dropsy. An ancient authority on herbs states that this herb is also valuable for bleeding at the mouth or nose. The preferred method of doing this would be to apply some of this herb in dry powdered form directly to the areas of bleeding.

ADRUE

Also known as Guinea Rush.

Botanical name: Cyperus articulatus.

Effects and reported uses: The aroma of this herb tends to reduce the desire for vomiting and is therefore recommended in conditions where it is desired that the patient retain the food taken. This includes the common vomiting of pregnancy as well as cases of imperfect digestion of food (dyspepsia). Of course, where food has been swallowed that is contaminated or poisonous or otherwise difficult to digest, it may be better to allow and even to encourage vomiting. This herb acts in the manner of a sedative and spreads a feeling of warmth throughout the system.

AGAR

Also known as agar-agar, Japanese Isinglass, vegetable gelatin, Japanese or Chinese Gelatin.

Botanical names: Gelidium amansii, Gelidium corneum of the family Gelidaceae.

Habitat: In Japan, Yellow and China Seas along the eastern coast of Asia, and in the Pacific Ocean, along the coast of California.

Description: This is an algae that is collected in the summer and autumn and usually spread out in the sun and allowed to bleach until dried. The substance is then boiled with water and the mucilaginous liquid separated by straining through a cloth. The liquid, after being cooled, is then cut into strips and dried by exposure to the air and sun, in a cold area to prevent growth of bacteria and molds. When one part of agar is boiled for ten minutes with one hundred parts of water and the product cooled, a stiff jelly results.

Effects: The protein content of agar gives it a nutritive character and one ounce of agar to twenty ounces of boiling water makes a suitable jelly for invalids. It is capable of taking up or absorbing two hundred times its volume of water to form a jelly. It is soothing and relieves inflammation.

Recorded uses: Powdered agar sprinkled on stewed fruits has been recommended for constipation. It is also available on the market as a vegetable gelatin and, when flavored, makes an excellent dessert. It has been often prescribed for the ill as a nutritive food easy to digest and tending to reduce conditions of constipation or congested bowels. It has been widely used in laboratories as a culture medium for research purposes and testing for the presence of bacteria. It is also used commercially in the making of some ice creams, candies and jellies. It is used as a mild laxative in a commercial preparation that combines agar with mineral oil and a mild stimulating laxative.

AGARIC

Also known as White Agaric, Larch Agaric, Purging Agaric.

Botanical names: Polyporus officinalis, boletus laricis.

Effects and reported uses: Checks and limits secretions of mucous membranes and glands, thus producing an astringent effect. When taken internally, the effect upon the bowels produces a cleansing result and this herb is therefore also a purgative. When taken in small quantities, there is no purgative or cleansing effect and instead the astringent effect is most noticeable. A small dose of approximately three grains or about one-half the size of a single seven-grain tablet is considered desirable for checking perspiration, diarrhea and for checking the secretion of milk in the mother after weaning. A large dose, from twenty to sixty grains, has a purgative effect.

AGRIMONY

Also known as Stickwort, Cocklebur.

Botanical name: Agrimonia eupatoria.

Habitat: Europe.

Growth needs: Fair amount of good soil, water and sunshine.

Description: This plant has small yellow flowers on a long spike. The leaves are hairy and are at least five inches long. The leaves are also narrow and pointed and the edges are toothed. This is a perennial plant, growing year after year.

Part used: Entire plant.

Effects: This herb has as astringent effect, as it contracts and hardens tissue. When absorbed into the system, this herb also strengthens and tones the muscles of the body and is therefore a tonic. Agrimony also affects the cells of the kidneys, allowing fluids to pass more readily through the kidneys, and it is therefore regarded as a diuretic.

Recorded uses: As in the case of other astringent herbs, the use of Agrimony tends to reduce or remove diarrhea. One old herbal refers to this herb as effective in improving the stomach, liver and bowels and has recommended it highly in the treatment of stones and gravel in the kidneys and bladder. This herb may also be used as a gargle for reducing soreness of the mouth and throat. Dried, it may be ground into powdered form and then used by mixing a teaspoonful of the powder into a cup of hot water, allowed to steep for a few minutes, and a cup of the mixture taken two or three times a day. A similar mixture has been recommended as a protection following snake bites or stings and an old herbal, published in 1640, recommends this plant for causing foreign objects in the flesh to be drawn out, such as thorns and wood splinters.

ALDER, BLACK, AMERICAN

Botanical name: Prinos verticillatus.

Effects and reported uses: The bark of this tree, after being steeped in hot water, produces a solution that has a strong laxative effect and has been highly recommended for constipation. The dosage would be approximately one-half to one teaspoon of the powdered bark to a cup of hot water.

ALDER, ENGLISH

**Known botanically as Alnus glu-
tinosa.**

Effects and uses: The leaves of this tree are useful in
applying to inflamed parts of the body. The bark, when
steeped in hot water, produces a mixture that has been used
as a tonic and as a gargle for sore throat. The mixture has
also been recommended as an astringent, as it tends to contract tissue and reduce secretion of fluids.

ALKANET

**Also known as Dyer's Bugloss,
Spanish Bugloss, Anchusa, Or-
chanet.**

Botanical names: Alkanna tinctoria, Lithospermum tinc-
torium, Anchusa tinctoria.

Effects and reported uses: This herb has the effect of
softening and soothing the parts of the body to which applied, being an emollient. The part used is the root. In addition to its emollient effect, this herb has the effect of contracting tissue and causing a cessation of flow of body
liquids. It is also said to have antiseptic qualities for treatment of wounds and, when taken internally, will destroy
body worms. The reported dosage is one-half teaspoon of

the powdered herb to a cup of hot water, in which the herb has been allowed to steep. The powder may be mixed in equal proportions with vaseline to make an ointment suitable for back pains or bruises.

ALL-HEAL

Also known as wound-wort.

Botanical name: Brunella vulgaris.

Effect and reported uses: This European plant has antiseptic qualities and in addition has the ability to relieve muscular spasms. These two qualities make the herb effective for relieving convulsions or other spasms. It has been found to be effective for destroying body worms and has been reported effective for the bites of dogs or other animals. It has also been recommended in cases of delay in the start of the menstrual period. The juice of the plant may be used with a dosage of five drops to one-half glass of hot water that has been cooled to allow drinking. Or, the plant may be dried and then powdered, after which one ounce of the powder to a pint of boiling water will produce a drink with an adequate amount of the herb in it. This may be taken two or three times daily.

ALLSPICE

Also known as Pimento, Jamaica Pepper.

Botanical name: Pimenta officinalis.

Effect and reported uses: The agreeable odor of this herb classes it as an aromatic. It is also a stomachic in that it excites activity in the stomach. It is a carminative in that it tends to remove gases from the upper intestinal tract. Inasmuch as it imparts flavor to almost any food, it is also a condiment. Allspice is often added to other herbs in the treatment of gas in the digestive tract or for indigestion generally. It is also useful in cases of diarrhea. The part of the herb that is used is the round brown fruits. After drying, a powder is usually made. The dosage sufficient for average use would be some powder equivalent to that of a seven-grain tablet or pill.

ALOES

Also known as Bombay Aloes, Turkey Aloes, Mocha Aloes, Zanzibar Aloes, Socotrine Aloe, Curacao Aloe, Bitter Aloe, Cape Aloe, Cape.

Botanical name: Liliacae Family; aloe socotrina.

Habitat: Africa (South). Also, Dutch West Indies.

Growth needs: Hot climate, fair amount of moisture, sun.

Description: There are several varieties of aloe plants. The Cape Aloe comes from the species known as Aloe Ferox. This plant may be as high as 20 feet with a trunk diameter of up to three feet. The leaves are lance-like in shape and are spiny. The leaves are cut and then the juice is allowed to trickle from the leaves. The juice is brought to a boil and thickened, then poured into containers and allowed to harden. When dried, it is ground into powder.

Part used: Exudate (moisture) of leaves of plant.

Effects: Acts as a purgative in constipation of the colon, having a tendency to drastically cleanse mucous membranes reached by it. In addition to the intestines, it also cleanses the stomach and serves to stimulate menstrual flow.

Recorded uses: Constipation relief, suppression of menstruation or inactive stomach. This herb has been known to expel pinworms from the intestines. Because of its powerful action, it is not recommended where there is a pregnancy or where there may be painful hemorrhoids. It should be avoided by a woman during her menstrual period. The average dose is four grains once or twice a day. In addition to taking this herb in compressed powder (tablet) form, the powder is soluble in both water and alcohol. The customary preparation is one ounce of the powder to a pint of the liquid. A teaspoonful of the solution would be sufficient for a single dose. A form of aloe is called Aloin, which is derived from a mixture of the aloe. It is used as a tonic laxative and as a purgative for the colon. A dose of one-quarter grain is the usual amount prescribed.

ALSTONIA BARK

Also known as Fever Bark, Australian Quinine, Australian Febrifuge.

Botanical name: Alstonia constricta.

Effect and reported uses: This is a favorite Australian tonic and agent for reducing fever. It also is rated as highly effective in some forms of rheumatism. The recommended dosage is from two to eight grains, depending upon the age of the patient and the severity of the illness. The dosage of herbs should be steeped in a cup of boiling water for several minutes after which the liquid may be swallowed.

AMARANTH

Also known as Red Cockscomb, Love-lies-bleeding.

Botanical names: Amaranthus hypochondriacus, Amaranthus melancholicus.

Effects and reported uses: This herb is an astringent, having the effect of contracting tissue and limiting secretion of glands. It has been recommended for excessive bleeding at the time of the menstrual period and is also recommended for diarrhea as well as bleeding from the bowels. A mixture may be prepared by adding an ounce of the powdered herb to a pint of boiling water. The mixture, after being cooled down to body temperature, may either be swallowed a cupful at a time two or three times a day or it may be used as an enema. The liquid is also useful as a wash for ulcers and sores and as a gargle for the throat and mouth.

AMMONIACUM

Also known as Persian Gum Ammoniacum.

Botanical name: Dorema Ammoniacum.

Effect and reported uses: This is a gum resin that is a natural exudation from the plant and serves as a stimulant, causing removal of the secretions of the bronchial passages. The gum, in powdered form, is steeped in hot water, one ounce to a pint of boiling water. Of particular value is the use of this preparation in asthmatic conditions involving spasms of the bronchial passages, as this herb is antispasmodic in its effect.

ANGELICA, EUROPEAN

Also known as Garden Angelica.

Botanical name: Angelica archangelica.

Effects and reported uses: This plant has a pleasing aromatic fragrance and is also stimulating to many functions of the body. When taken internally, this herb has a tendency to reduce gas conditions in the intestines and because of the effect on the kidneys tends to increase the production of urine. It also promotes perspiration. The powdered root of this herb, in the proportion of one ounce to a pint of boiling water, produces a drink that has been found to be valuable in various lung diseases including coughs and shortness of the breath. It also has the effect of opening passages in the liver and spleen, allowing these organs to function better. The drink has also been recommended for indigestion, especially when due to excessive indulgence in food. Because of the ability of this herb to clear tiny passages, it has been used to relieve dimness of vision and hearing by placing drops of the fluid into the eyes and ears. It is also reported as being capable of relieving toothache. An important reported use of this herb is taking either the fluid or the powder itself and applying it directly to ulcerous wounds or sores of the body when other methods have failed. It is reported that this herb heals ulcers and helps restore the normal tissues. Another valuable use of this herb is in the case of the gout when applications of the liquid directly to the places of pain have been reported to give relief.

ANGUSTURA

Also known as Cusparia Bark.

Botanical names: Cusparia febrifuga, Galipea officinalis, Bonplandia trifoliata, Galipea cusparia.

Habitat, effects and reported uses: Originating in and native plant of Venezuela, this herb has an agreeable and

spicy odor and is therefore an aromatic plant. It stimulates
functional body activity and is considered to have a tonic
effect. It has been recommended for diarrhea, intermittent
fevers and for conditions where there has been an accumulation of water in the tissues and cavities. An average dose
would vary between five and fifteen grains of the powdered
bark. Any larger quantity could cause vomiting and a
watery evacuation of the intestinal contents.

ANISE

**This herb is also referred to
as Anise Seed, Aniseed, Sweet
Cumin and Anisum.**

Botanical name: Pimpinella Anisum Linne or Pimpinella anisum. The French name for this herb is Anis and the
German name is Anissame.

Habitat: While well known in Asia and in southern
Europe, where Anise has been in use for many centuries,
it is also cultivated in many areas of the United States as
a garden plant, notably in the state of Rhode Island. Supplies of Anise used in the United States are obtained either
from domestic sources in the United States or from Mexico.

Growth needs: The soil should be moderately rich, well
drained and sandy. Seeds are sown in early spring directly
into the field. When seedlings are two to three inches high,
they are thinned out so as to be about eight inches apart.
This plant will apparently not grow in a dry or arid area

unless amply watered. Being an annual plant, the temperature is not very important, just so there is at least one growing season.

Description: The stem of this herb rises to a height of approximately 13 inches, the stem being erect, cylindrical and smooth. The stem is striated, meaning that it is striped with marks. The flowers are small and white in color, each on a long hairy stalk or pedicel. The fruit (seed) is mouse-shaped with a sharp-pointed head, relatively large body and tail or stem. This plant has upper leaves and lower leaves. The leaves at the upper part of the plant grow opposite each other on the stem, while the lower leaves grow alternately. The lower leaves have long stems while the upper leaves have short stems holding the leaves. The lower leaves are ovate (egg shaped) with a pointed apex while the upper leaves are feather-like in shape.

Physiological effect: There are numerous globules of oil in this herb which, upon inhalation or other absorption into the body, has a stimulating effect. The oil is not unpleasant and is therefore used as a flavoring agent also.

Conditions for which anise has been recommended:

Cases of gas in the stomach or bowels, known as flatulence.

It is also used as a stimulant for vital organs of the body such as the heart, liver, lungs, brain, etc.

As a hot tea, anise will check pains in the bowels due to over-distention of the bowels caused by gas formation.

FLAVORING: This is often mixed with other foods or herbs to give a palatable taste and flavor.

FOR CHILDREN: This herb has been popular for many years with children, for flatulence or for colic due to hasty or excessive eating.

PREPARATION: For children, it may be given in doses of one or two drops on lumps of sugar or fruit. For adults, the dose may be from one-half to one fluid ounce. This is a harmless herb and may be taken as often as desired without fear of any injury.

OTHER USES: The anise seed oil is often used with cough medicines to sweeten the taste and produce a fragant odor.

ARBUTUS, TRAILING

**Also known as Gravel Plant,
Ground Laurel, Mountain Pink,
Winter Pink, Mayflower.**

Botanical name: Epigae repens.

Effect and reported uses: This herb, being an astringent, has the effect of contracting and hardening tissue and checking secretions of mucous membranes. It has been found to be especially valuable in cases of weak bladders or bladders containing so-called gravel or crystalline dust or concretions of crystal, sometimes referred to as bladder stones. The use of this herb has been recommended when the urine contains blood or pus. One ounce of the leaves in a pint of boiling water makes an infusion that may be taken freely several times a day for best results.

ARECA NUT

Also known as Betel Nut.

Botanical name: Areca Catechu.

Effects and reported uses: This herb contracts and hardens tissue and checks secretions of mucous membranes, being an astringent. It has been recommended as a remedy for expelling tapeworms. The nut is powdered and administered in a dosage of one teaspoon mixed with some sugary syrup for easier administration, followed by a purgative such as castor oil that will cause a watery evacuation of the bowels.

ARENARIA RUBRA

Also known as Sandwort.

Botanical names: Lepigonum rubrum, Tissa rubra, Buda rubra.

Effects and reported uses: This herb acts as a diuretic, stimulating functioning of the bladder, and is especially known in Malta for this use. It has been recommended for inflammation of the bladder, known as cystitis, as well as for bladder stones. The powdered herb is allowed to steep

in a pint of boiling water in the proportion of one ounce
of the powder to a pint of water. It has been recommended
to be taken several times a day, perhaps a cup every two
hours until relief is obtained. This should be accompanied
by a mild diet with non-irritating foods such as barley water.

ARNICA

Botanical name: Arnica montana.

Effects and reported uses: This herb serves as a stimulant, increasing functional activity of the organs of the body.
It is also a favorite remedy for applying directly to wounds
for healing purposes, and is also valuable for bruises and
swellings. It should not be taken internally as severe and
fatal cases of poisoning are on record. The entire plant is
dried and after drying, the herb is reduced to powder. It is
then mixed in equal portions with vaseline or mineral oil
and applied to the body parts in need of care.

ARRACH

Also known as Stinking Arrach, Goosefoot.

Botanical name: Chenopodium olidum.

Effects and reported uses: This herb acts as a sedative
for the nerves, lessening the irritability of nerves and increasing nerve energy. Because of this quality, this herb has
been widely used for nerves, especially in cases of hysteria
or high nerve tension. Another valuable use for this herb

is in connection with stimulation of the menstrual function due to obstructions in the flow. The proportion is one ounce of the powdered herb to a pint of boiling water. After the infusion is cooled sufficiently to drink, it may be taken internally. Usually, two or three cups of the solution per day has been found adequate for good results.

ARROWROOT

Also known as Bermuda Arrowroot, Maranta, Natal Arrowroot, St. Vincent Arrowroot.

Botanical name: Maranta arundinacea.

Effects and reported uses: The root of this plant is used, particularly the starch obtained from the root. This can be made into a nutritive drink especially for infants and convalescents. From two to three teaspoonfuls of the white powdered root may be boiled in a pint of water, and the drink may be taken several times a day. Instead of boiling in water, the herb may be boiled in milk. It may be seasoned with the usual flavoring ingredients such as lemon juice or fruits. The herb has a soothing and softening effect upon mucous membranes, in addition to being nutritious.

ASAFETIDA

**Devil's Dung, Food of the Gods
Also known as Gum Asafetida,**

Botanical name: Umbelliferae, Ferula foetida Regel, Ferula Assa-foetida Linne.

Habitat: Persia (Iran) and Afghanistan. It is also grown in India.

Growth needs: Hot climate, sandy soil and fair amount of moisture.

Description: A short perennial herb, with a conical erect rhizome (stem between root and leaves). The stem is green and soft. The leaves are divided into three distinct segments (ternate). The flowers are yellow. To obtain the gum-resin, the stems are cut down and a slice cut from the head of the rhizome. In about a month, the collectors return and find a thick, reddish, gummy exudate which is scraped off and placed into containers. The exudate is then allowed to harden in the sun.

Part used: The exudate or gum-resin.

Effects: Stimulant to the brain and nervous system, expectorant, tonic, laxative, diuretic (urine producing), diaphoretic (produces perspiration), emmenagogue (stimulates menstrual flow), aphrodisiac (increasing sexual desires) and anthelmintic (tending to expel intestinal worms).

Recorded uses: The average dose of from five to twenty grains of the powdered gum-resin stimulates the circulation and raises blood pressure. An ounce of the powder in a pint of boiling water makes an emulsion which, when cooled, may be taken in small quantities (tablespoonful as an average dose) to produce results and the effects listed above. The emulsion has been found valuable in cases of excessive air in the stomach of infants, causing the pain known as colic. It has been reportedly used as an enema in cases of convulsions involving infants. It has been found useful for croup and relieves stomach irritation, hysteria and spasmodic nervous diseases. This herb produces a sensation of warmth without any rise in body temperature. It has been highly praised as an aid in the prevention of miscarriage, mildly stimulating both ovarian and intestinal activity. The taste is objectionable but in Asia, where it is a common food supplement, a taste for this herb has been acquired over a period of time.

ASARABACCA

Also known as Hazelwort, Wild Nard.

Botanical name: Asarum Europaeum.

Effects and reported uses: The root of this herb is used as an emetic, inducing vomiting, and is said to be in popular use in France for this purpose. The quantity should not exceed what is equivalent to one or two seven-grain tablets or a purgative effect is likely to occur resulting in a free watery evacuation of the intestinal contents. For a purgative effect, an amount of powder equal to approximately five to ten seven-grain tablets would ordinarily be necessary.

ASH

**Also known as Common Ash,
European Ash, Weeping Ash.**

Botanical name: Fraxinus excelsior

Effects and reported uses: The bark and leaves of this
herb are used as a laxative when taken in a small quantity,
not exceeding ten grains, and become a cleansing purgative
when taken in slightly larger quantity such as from twenty
to thirty grains. The bark of the plant, steeped in hot water,
makes a drink considered in some countries ideal for fever,
especially malarial fever. The leaves of this herb have been
used with success in cases of inflammation of and pain in
the great toe (gout), as well as inflammation of joints generally (arthritis and rheumatism). An ounce of the leaves
may be steeped in a pint of boiling water, allowed to cool
somewhat, and then taken several times a day, one-half cup
at a time.

ASPARAGUS

Botanical name: Asparagus officinalis.

Effects and reported uses: This commonly used plant
has long been popular as a side dish with meals, but it also
has special healing properties. Not only has it been highly
recommended as a diuretic for stimulation of action of the

kidneys, but also as a mild laxative and as a sedative for the nervous system. It has also been recommended for cases of enlarged heart and for conditions involving accumulation to an excessive degree of fluids in tissues and in body cavities. For health purposes, it is best to take the fresh asparagus and express or extract the juice therefrom in doses of a tablespoonful at a time several times a day.

AVENS

Also known as Colewort, Herb Bennet.

Botanical names: Geum urbanum, Radix caryophyllata.

Effects and reported uses: This plant, including the root, has an astringent effect, in that it checks secretions of the mucous membranes and contracts and hardens tissue. It is especially valuable for its effect in contracting blood vessels so as to stop hemorrhages, thus having a styptic effect. It is also a tonic as it has been reported successful in restoring power and strength in cases of weakness and debility. It has also been found useful in cases of diarrhea, tending to diminish constant watery discharges from the intestines. The drinking of an infusion of one ounce of the powdered herb steeped in a pint of boiling water is also reported to be helpful for women suffering from leucorrhea, a disease marked by the discharge of a greenish-white mucus from the female genital passages. A cup of the drink may be taken for the foregoing effects several times a day, usually in the morning, at noon and in the evening.

AZADIRACHTA

Also known as Nim, Margosa,
Neem.

Botanical name: Melia Azadirachta.

Effects and reported uses: This herb has been widely
used in the southern part of the United States as an agent
for expelling worms from the intestinal tract. Usually, the
drink is prepared by taking four ounces of the bark and
boiling it in a quart of water until the solution is reduced
to one pint. The dose is a tablespoonful every three hours.
It is best to accompany the dose with some purgative soon
afterwards to cleanse the system, such as castor oil or cascara sagrada. This herb has some purgative value as well
as the trait of destroying intestinal worms (anthelmintic),
but it is best to use some well-known purgative in addition
to this herb. By taking an ounce of the powder and mixing
it in a cup of water, this produces an emetic or vomiting
effect.

BAEL

Also known as Bel, Indian Bael,
Bengal Quince.

Botanical name: Aegle Marmelos.

Effects and uses: The unripe fruit of this herb has the effect of contracting tissue and reducing the flow of liquids or fluids from the glands. It is well known in India as a remedy for diarrhea and it is reported as non-constipating. It is recommended for other ailments where there is inflammation of mucous membrane accompanied by ulcers or fever or both.

BALM

Also known as Sweet Balm,
Lemon Balm, Garden Balm,
Common Balm.

Botanical name: Melissa Officinalis of the Family Labiatae.

Habitat: Southern Europe, Middle East and Northern Africa. Also cultivated in the United States.

Growth needs: Requires considerable water and sunshine. Soil need be only fairly nutritious. It is easily grown from seed.

Description: A small tree with a pungent lemon scent in early spring. Leaves grow on the stem opposite to each other, broad and round with hairy leaves. The flowers are pale yellow.

Parts used: The dried leaves with or without the flowering tops.

Effects: Produces perspiration (diaphoretic); also soothing and calming to nerves.

Recorded uses: A handful of leaves, dried or fresh, may be steeped in hot water for ten minutes and sweetened with honey to make a refreshing tea. It has been highly recommended in cases of feverish colds. It has an astringent or tightening action on tissues so as to stop or slow discharge from mucous membranes. It is also recommended for relieving headaches. It may be taken cold by pouring a pint of boiling water over an ounce of the herb, allowing it to stand for about fifteen minutes, then letting it cool. It is then strained and may be taken freely by feverish patients to relieve the fever. It has a taste and odor like lemon. When taken cold, it relieves fever; when taken hot, it produces perspiration. It has also been used and recommended for painful or suppressed menstruation. It is also reported to be valuable as an aid in digestion and for relief in case of nausea or vomiting. It has also been recommended for troubles involving the liver, spleen, kidneys and bladder. Another recorded use is for relief of boils, the herb being made into a warm poultice and allowed to soak over the boil overnight. It will usually bring the boil to a head and cause it to break. The poultice may also be used for insect stings in conjunction with drinking of the tea at the same time. One of the herbals also recommends similar treatment for dog bites. This herb has also been recommended for toothache, using the combination treatment method of applying the herb to the tooth and drinking the tea.

BALM OF GILEAD

Botanical name: Populus candicans.

Effects and reported uses: This herb stimulates the body organs and also has nutritive value, therefore being both a stimulant and a tonic. The buds of this plant are allowed to dry and then ground into powder. A dose of from five to ten grains of the powder is an adequate amount and is especially recommended by herb authorities as excellent for ailments of the chest, lungs, stomach and kidneys. When mixed with a small amount of vaseline, the ointment has been found helpful for colds and pains in the chest and especially for various skin diseases. The ointment has also been found useful for relieving the pains of rheumatism and the gout.

BALMONY

Also known as Bitter Herb, Snake Head, Turtle Head, Turtle Bloom.

Botanical name: Chelone glabra.

Effects and reported uses: This herb has many uses. It is a tonic, giving strength to the tissues; it is an anthelmintic, relieving the intestinal tract of worms; it is a detergent, in that it purges and cleanses areas reached by this herb; and it is antibilious, being a remedy for disordered conditions of the liver that cause constipation, headache, loss of appetite and vomiting of bile. It is especially recommended for worms in children. An ounce of the powdered leaf can be steeped in a pint of boiling water. After some cooling, the drink may be taken frequently in doses of one-half cup every two or three hours.

BAMBOO BRIER

Also known as Wild Sarsaparilla.

Botanical name: Aralia nudicaulis.

Effects and reported uses: The root of this plant is used as an alterative, that is, it alters the processes of nutrition and excretion, restoring the normal functions of the system. It has a tonic effect, increasing the strength and tone of body tissue, and has been successful in cases of rheumatism as well as diseases of the skin, this herb being recognized as a blood purifier. It has been widely used in constitutional tuberculosis characterized by glandular swelling in the neck and inflammations of joints and mucous membranes. Dosage is equivalent to approximately two seven-grain tablets of the powdered root taken two or three times daily, or an ounce of the powder may be steeped in a pint of boiling water and the drink taken freely several times a day.

BARBERRY

Also known as Berberis, Oregon-
grape Root, Trailing Mahonia,
Rocky Mountain Grape, Ber-
beritze, Berberina.

Botanical name: Berberis Linne; berberis vulgaris; berberis aquifolium.

Growth needs: Grows on the mountain ranges of the
Pacific coast area and especially in Oregon, Washington and
California. It is a hardy shrub and requires little care other
than reasonable amounts of rain and sunshine.

Habitat: Western coast of United States.

Description: Woody shrub with smooth stems of yellowish gray color. The flowers are yellow. Cork stem de-
taches in long strips. Leaves are small with teeth-like edges
and with spines.

Parts used: The bark, berries and rootbark. Also, the
stem below the ground.

Effects: In small doses, it is an astringent bitter, a tonic
and stomach aid. In large doses, it is cathartic, producing
watery diarrhea with abdominal pain. It is said to have
considerable alterative powers, changing nutritive processes
to a normal state. When used in moderate amounts, it has

been used as a remedy for typhoid fever, diarrhea and dyspepsia (indigestion). Relieves pain, soreness and burning sensations along the biliary ducts (containing bile) as well as the urinary tracts.

Recorded uses:

As a bitter tonic, for general improvement of vitality; as a remedy for liver and spleen conditions; chronic ailments of the stomach; early stages of tuberculosis; control running from bronchial tubes (secretions); used as a treatment for syphilis; antiseptic uses for destroying disease germs.

Preparations and dosages: The berries make a pleasant acid drink effective in cases of diarrhea and fevers. The bark in powdered form may be taken three to four times daily in quantities of one-quarter teaspoonful. No harmful results have been reported from the use of this herb.

BARLEY

**Also known as Pearl Barley,
Perlatum.**

Botanical name: Hordeum distichon, of the Family Graminaceae.

Habitat: Believed to have originated in western Asia, barley being one of the most ancient foods of the human race. Large supplies are now produced in the United States, Soviet Union, India, Germany, Roumania, Japan and Spain.

Growth needs: The growth of barley requires good soil, with ample water and a fair amount of sunshine.

Description: Barley is an annual grain reaching a height of from two to three feet. The stem has alternate leaves with pronounced auricles (ear appendages). The straw-stem of this grass (the culm) usually has five to seven joints and sometimes eight joints. Threshing separates the grain from the straw. The barley kernel resembles the wheat kernel except that the groove of the barley kernel is broad and shallow.

Part used: The decorticated seed. (After removed from husk.)

Effects: Nutritive food, containing protein (8 to 19 percent), starch, enzymes and vitamins. Believed to contain all the essential nutrients.

Recorded uses: Barley is valuable as food for the sick and convalescent. In addition, this food is soothing to irritated surfaces, and is therefore valuable as a diet for conditions where it is desirable for food to be easily digested. By taking two ounces of the barley grains (referred to as barleycorns) and, after washing them, pouring a pint of cold water on them and boiling for twenty minutes, then allowing the decoction to cool, the barley-water remaining is a non-irritating food ideal for children suffering from diarrhea or inflammatory conditions of the bowels or other inflammatory conditions of mucous membranes of the body. The barley seed is also used to manufacture malt, a source of beer, ale and whiskey. By-products of the malt, after beer-making, are used mainly for cattle feed. Sometimes the barley seeds are roasted and used as a coffee substitute. Another use for barley is to prepare it as soup, giving nourishment quickly and without any strain on the digestive system.

BEARSFOOT, AMERICAN

Also known as Uvedalia, Leaf Cup, Yellow Leaf Cup.

Botanical name: Polymnia Uvedalia.

Effects and reported uses: The root of this herb acts to stimulate the glands of the body and produces a laxative effect as well as a pain relieving effect, serving as an anodyne. There have been reports of its high value in cases of liver and spleen congestive conditions. The herb has also been found of value in cases of inflammation of glands associated with liver and spleen conditions. It also aids in digestive conditions known as dyspepsia, especially hepatic dyspepsia, resulting from liver disease. An authority also recommends this herb as a hair tonic for direct application to the scalp or mixing the herb with lanolin and applying it to the scalp as an ointment. While the herb may be effective in powdered form, it is more conveniently used in the form of a fluid extract, the herb being soaked in water or alcohol and the qualities of the herb extracted into the fluid. Dosage would be from fifteen to sixty drops of the extract taken several times a day. As this herb has a faintly bitter taste, it may be taken with honey or other agreeable substance.

BELLADONNA

Also known as Deadly Nightshade, Dwale, Black Cherry Root.

Botanical name: Atropa Belladonna.

Habitat: United States, Central Europe, England and India.

Growth needs: The best soil is deep, well-drained, moist loam. In area where frost freezes the ground, it is best to remove the plant in the fall, keeping it indoors and replanting it in the spring. Two crops of leaves can be gathered from plants during the first year.

Description: The root is pale brown, about three-quarters of an inch in diameter, and six or more inches long. The leaves are somewhat round or sphere-shaped, with smooth edges and slightly hairy. The flower is yellowish-purple.

Parts used: Root and leaves.

Effects: The root or leaves of this herb serve as a diuretic, increasing the secretion of urine. It also serves as an anodyne, relieving pain, and relaxes overcontracted smooth muscle and is therefore a sedative. It depresses sensory nerve endings.

Recorded uses: Widely used in conditions accompanied by a rise in temperature such as night-sweats. Also it is used where there is insufficient flow of urine due to sluggish kidneys. It is often prescribed as a pain reliever, and seems to be effective in relieving coughs or whooping coughs. Its action also makes it effective in the condition involving loss of semen involuntarily, known as spermatorrhea. Despite its sedative action, this herb is also known to be valuable for stimulating the circulation. It is also recognized as an antidote where poisoning has resulted from the use of various depressants such as opium. It is also widely used in connection with rheumatic inflammation and in cases of gout, relieving both the pain and inflammation. In such cases, there is an external application of the liquid directly to the affected parts.

BENNE

Also know as Sesam, Gingelly, Sesame.

Botanical name: Sesamum indicum.

Effects and reported uses: The leaves and seeds of this herb are used as a demulcent and as a laxative. By steeping the fresh leaves in hot water, the resulting drink, largely used by Indians as a tea, relieves catarrhal conditions. These conditions, usually involving the mucous membrane of the lungs and bronchial tubes, if not relieved, generally result or are already associated with emphysema or asthma. By its demulcent effect, this herb, in its tea form, may be applied directly to the skin where the skin has erupted or is bruised, having a soothing and softening effect. It has also been used by Indians in various opthalmic (eye) complaints such as inflammation or soreness. The seeds of this plant have an oil having effects similar to olive oil and may be used for the same purposes. The oil has a laxative effect and the leaves have an opposite effect, being used to combat diarrhea. The solution from the leaves, described above, is also used for dysentery. the inflammation of the large intestine with bloody and loose evacuations. A distinct characteristic of the oil of the seeds is that when taken internally it will usually hasten and facilitate the menstrual period.

BENZOIN

Also known as Gum Benjoin, Gum Benjamin, Siam Benzoin, Sumatra Benzoin, Palembang Benzoin, Benzoin Laurel, Benjamin Tree.

Botanical names: Styrax Benzoin, Styrax Benzoin Dryander, Styrax Tonkinensis.

Effects and reported uses: The herb is prepared in two forms, the dry powder formed from hardened and dried sap exudation and the tincture, with the exudate dissolved into alcohol. The herb is used both internally and externally. The effect of internal use is to expel mucus from the throat or lungs. It is known as a stimulating expectorant because of the stimulating effect of the herb upon the tissues. It is valuable for coughs and bronchitis and is often used in cough medicines. Externally, it may be applied directly to wounds, sores or other ailments or sores of tissues. It is an antiseptic as well as a stimulant.

BERBERIS

Botanical name: Berberis aristata.

Effects and reported uses: This has been commonly used in India as a bitter tonic for intermittent fevers. The action of this herb is similar to the herb Golden Seal. The dosage is from ten to sixty grains of the dry herb in powdered form. See the section on Golden Seal for the use of this herb in view of the similar action.

BETH ROOT

**Also known as Birthroot,
Lamb's Quarter.**

Botanical names: Trillium pendulum, Trillium erectum.

Effects and reported uses: This herb checks secretions of the mucous membrane and so it is an astringent. It is found effective in relieving chest conditions such as coughs, and so it is also a pectoral. It restores normal functions of nutrition and excretion and thus qualifies as an alterative, and it increases strength and tone of muscle and so it is also a tonic. It is reported valuable in cases of internal bleeding, including profuse menstruation, and is effective in many lung or pulmonary complaints. This herb is often used as an ingredient in solutions for enemas, both for rectal irrigation and for treatment of female organs. It is found especially valuable as an astringent for the organs of the uterus and in cases where there is a whitish viscous discharge from the vagina and uterine cavity, the condition known as leucorrhea. An infusion is made by pouring a pint of boiling water over a tablespoonful of the powder of the root of the herb. This may be taken freely in doses of one-half cup or more when it is to be used as an astringent. Three or four times a day should be adequate. For coughs or similar problems, about ten to twenty grains of the powdered root may be taken in a little water three times a day. This herb may be mixed with equal parts of Slippery Elm to obtain a good antiseptic poultice for open areas. A small quantity of powdered Lobelia Seed may be added to the mixture for more effect.

BILBERRIES

Also known as Huckleberries, Whortleberries, Hurtleberries.

Botanical name: Vaccinium Myrtillus.

Effects and reported uses: The ripe berry fruit as well as the dried berry is used. When the ripe fruit is eaten, it acts to relieve fever and thirst and is therefore described as a cooling nutriment. The dried berries have been found to be valuable in cases of accumulation of fluids in cavities, a condition known as dropsy. It is also found valuable in easing cases of formation of so-called gravel formations in the kidneys or bladder. A pint of boiling water poured over an ounce of the dried berries will produce a drink effective for diarrhea and inflammation or derangements of the bowels. This may be taken several times a day by mouth and the same solution may be used as an enema for direct contact with the intestinal tract. Another solution for drinking during typhoid epidemics, for both prevention and treatment, is to take a pound of the bilberries and boil for twenty minutes in one gallon of water, adding one-quarter pound of Cream of Tartar during the boiling. The solution is then strained and the liquid may be taken several times a day a cupful at a time. The same solution will be helpful in stimulating the flow of urine as a diuretic, and it may be used as a gargle for sore throat. It may also be used externally for washing of open wounds, sores and ulcers. It is also valuable for an enema or for washing of the female tract to treat leucorrhea, the whitish viscous discharge from the vagina and uterus.

BIRCH, EUROPEAN

Also known as White Birch.

Botanical name: Betula alba.

Effects and reported uses: This herb increases the tone of the gastro-intestinal mucous membrane and is therefore known as a bitter. By contracting tissue and arresting discharge of fluids, it is also an astringent. An ounce of the dried leaves may be steeped in hot water to produce a pint of solution that may be taken several times a day for the stomach and intestines. The bark of this tree yields a tar, from which is derived a volatile oil by distillation, known as Oleum Rusci or Oleum betulinum. This oil has been used internally for the treatment of gonorrhea but is more widely known as a remedy for skin diseases, especially those of the type known as eczema where there is itching, redness or infiltration, a condition where the skin contains deposits of diseased fluid.

BIRTHWORT

Botanical name: Aristolochia longa.

Effects and reported uses: The dried root of this herb is ground into powder and a dosage of from thirty to sixty grains is adequate for stimulation of functions of various glands and blood circulation. It has been especially recommended for relieving conditions of rheumatism or the gout. It has a spicy fragrance and so is termed an aromatic.

BISTORT

Also known as Snakeweed, Adderwort.

Botanical name: Polygonum bistorta.

Effects and reported uses: The root of this herb is used

as an astringent, as it tends to contract tissues and diminish fluid discharges. It is used chiefly to halt hemorrhages as well as other discharges of fluid. It is often taken by mouth but is also used as a gargle and used as injections in the form of enemas. The powdered root is mixed with water in proportions of ten to fifteen grains to a pint of water. If taken internally, the dosage is one tablespoonful twice daily, and more often if results are not obtained within two or three days.

BITTERSWEET

Also known as Woody Nightshade, Violet Bloom, Scarlet
Berry, Felonwood, Felonwort.

Botanical name: Solanum dulcamara.

Effects and reported uses: The twigs of this herb have the effect of subsiding swelling or inflammation and softening the area of the swelling. It is especially valuable in cases of rheumatism and it has the effect of causing obstinate eruptions of the skin to be cleared. Dosage is one-half to two ounces at a time several times a day with an equal quantity of milk. The drink is prepared by placing approximately one-quarter cup of the powdered twigs into two pints of boiling water boiled down to one pint. This solution has also been found valuable in cases of removal and/or improvement of abscesses due to tubercular diseases of lymphatic glands.

BITTERSWEET, AMERICAN

Also known as Waxwork, False
Bittersweet.

Botanical name: Celastrus scandens.

Effects and reported uses: Both the root and the bark
of this herb are used for several valuable effects. It is an
alterative in that it restores normal functions of nutrition
and excretion. It is also a diuretic in that it stimulates the
kidneys to excrete more urine. It is also a diaphoretic because it brings about perspiration. Bittersweet has been
used effectively in liver ailments tending to bring about an
alteration of the condition of the liver so that it will function normally. It has also been found valuable in cases of
leucorrhea, the condition of the female organs where there
is a whitish thick discharge from the female organs of reproduction. Where delayed menstruation occurs, this herb has
also been found effective. The drink is made by adding a
pint of boiling water to one ounce of the powdered root
or bark. Two to four ounces of the drink three times a day
has been found effective.

BLACKBERRY

Also known as American Blackberry, Bramble, Rubus, Sand
Blackberry, Dewberry, Gout
Berry, Cloud Berry, Bramble-
berry, Rubi Fructus.

Botanical name: Rubus Villosus, of the rose family, Rosaceae.

Habitat: United States and Europe.

Growth needs: Good soil, water and sunshine.

Description: Blackberries are shrubby and prickly plants growing in long and tough bands, the diameter being from three to six millimeters in thickness. The fruit is juicy and pleasantly flavored.

Part used: Fruit, bark of rhizome and roots and leaves.

Effects: The berry fruit is a popular food and has long been a remedy for loose bowels, especially for children during the summer months. The bark, root and leaves are just as valuable for loose bowels and similar conditions such as dysentery (inflammation of the large intestine). This plant has both an astringent and a tonic effect. It contracts tissues, reducing secretions.

Recorded uses: Highly esteemed in relieving diarrhea. To prepare, pour cold water on ground or bruised root, bark or leaves and boil for twenty minutes to one-half hour. Cool and strain. Use one ounce of the herb to one pint of water. An additional half-pint of water may be added to allow for the boiling away. The average dose is from two teaspoonfuls to one cup. It has also been used as an invigorating tonic.

BLACK CURRANT

Latin name: Ribes Nigrum of the Saxifragacae family.

Habitat: United States and Europe, especially northern England and Scotland.

Growth needs: Sun and fair soil.

Description: Low shrub. Leaves shaped as the palm of the hand (palmate) with five or more lobes. Yellow glands on under surface of leaves about two inches in diameter.

Effects and reported uses: The fruit is used for jams and jellies. The leaves are diuretic (stimulating urine excretion), reduce abnormal heat of the body (refrigerant), and act as a detergent, cleansing wounds and ulcers. Used for hoarse throats and as a tonic. The juice of the Black Currant berry has become known as an antiseptic and as a purifier of the blood. It has been used to restore the nervous system and it is valuable in anemia, malnutrition and general debility. This herb has a rich supply of vitamins and has considerable nutritive value.

To make a syrup of Black Currant, cover the leaves with boiling water and steep for one hour. Strain out the liquid and add honey. Boil the solution into a syrup and place in bottles for use as desired. Use about an ounce of the leaves to a pint of water. The amount of honey to be included depends upon the degree of sweetness desired.

BLACK HAW

Also known as Stagbush, American Sloe, Vibernum Prunifolium.

Botanical name: Caprifoliacae. Viburnum rufidulum Rafinesque.

Habitat: Eastern and mid-west United States, particularly in North Carolina and Tennessee.

Growth needs: These are hardy trees that will grow in almost any climate, provided there is a fair amount of water and fairly good soil.

Description: This plant is a shrub or small tree attaining a height of about fifteen feet. The leaves grow opposite each other on the stem and are slender and smooth with the edges of the leaves being saw-like in appearance. The flowers are white and the fruit is bluish-black, oval-shaped, sweet and edible.

Parts used: Dried bark of the root or stem.

Effects: Acts to normalize the uterus. Draws together soft organic tissue.

Recorded uses: Long used as a tonic for the uterus, to prevent painful menstruation (dysmenorrhea) as well as to relieve pains of menstruation. It has also been used for relief from the pains of childbirth and also to prevent miscarriages. It has been used to check bleeding from the uterus. The ordinary dosage is a tablespoonful every four hours. A pint of the herb is made by taking an ounce of the bark and soaking it thoroughly in a pint of hot water, just below the boiling point. This may take fifteen or twenty minutes of soaking or steeping. This drink also acts on the kidneys to encourage the production of urine, but the principal use of this herb is during pregnancy, for the treatment and especially for the prevention of nervous diseases of pregnancy. The usual dosage for the powdered bark is sixty grains, taken twice daily.

BLACK WILLOW BARK

**Also known as Pussy Willow,
Calkins Willow, and Marsh.**

Botanical names: Salix nigra, Salix discolor. Salicacea Family.

Habitat: Originally a European plant but naturalized to some extent in North America.

Growth needs: Average amount of rainfall, fair climate and good soil.

Description: Approximately six inches tall, the bark pieces are about three-quarters of an inch broad with a blackish gray exterior. There are numerous dark brown spots on the bark (lenticels). The taste is bitter, with no odor.

Part used: Bark and berries.

Effects: Astringent and antiseptic.

Recorded uses: This herb has special application to the reproductive organs.

FOR WOMEN: Referred to as the "woman's remedy," this herb is valuable for the inflamed and ulcerated surfaces of the mucous membrane of the vagina. The bark, in powdered form, is mixed (one ounce) with a pint of boiling water and used as a douche. The same solution may be taken for the relief of ovarian pain, the dosage being one ounce twice daily.

FOR MEN: Highly regarded in cases of nocturnal (nightly) involuntary emissions, also known as "wet dreams."

FOR BOTH MEN AND WOMEN: This herb serves as a sexual sedative (anaphrodisiac) where there is sexual irritation of the organs resulting from various genito-urinary irritations. By relieving the irritation, the desire for excessive sex relations is diminished.

OTHER USES: The powdered bark is excellent for direct application to areas of the skin where there are indolent (inactive) ulcers or gangrene. The powder may also be mixed with cream to make a poultice and used as such after being brought to a boil and allowed to simmer for a few minutes. The herb has also been effective for rheumatism, inflamed joints, muscles and nerves, using the same solution and dosage as above described.

BLOODROOT

**Also known as Sanguinaria, Red
Puccoon, Indian Red Paint, Tet-
terwort, Red Root, Indian Plant,
Pauson, Red Paint Root.**

Botanical name: Papaveraceae family; Latin name, Sanguinaria canadensis.

Habitat: Grows in North America, mainly in rich forest
soil.

Growth needs: Rich soil; ample water, warmth and sunshine.

Description: This is a low growing perennial herb. The
leaves have from seven to nine lobes with red-colored veins.
There is a large white flower with eight to twelve white
petals.

Part used: The dried rhizome (between underground
root and the leaves).

Preparation: The rhizome and roots should be collected
in the early spring and carefully dried. This is then ground
into a powder. The powder may be placed in capsules or
compressed into pill form.

Effects: A small dose (1/12th grain) serves as an expectorant, tending to loosen and detach from mucous mem-

brane loose fragments and loose phlegm. A smaller dose (1/20th grain) stimulates gastric and intestinal secretions.

Recorded uses:

1. GASTRIC (STOMACH) TONIC: Small dose.
2. CHEST DISEASES: Use expectorant dose. Has been successfully used in bleeding of the lungs, pneumonia, chronic bronchitis, whooping cough, croup, rhinitis (inflammation and running of the nose), sore throat, colds, laryngitis, typhoid fever, jaundice.
3. INHALANT: May be used as a snuff in small doses for treatment of stalk-like tumors growing from the mucous membrane of the nose. *Warning:* Large doses will produce narcotic effect.
4. EXTERNAL REMEDY: Powdered root effective for surface tumors, ringworm or wounds, including running sores. May be used in ointment form, for external uses. One preparation is an ounce of the root powder in three ounces of lard, the two items brought to a boil and allowed to simmer for several minutes, then strained.

BLUE FLAG

Also known as Water Flag, Poison Flag, Flag Lily, Liver Lily, Snake Lily, Larger Blue Flag, Water flay, Water lily, Flower-de-luce, Iris.

Botanical name: Iris versicolor of the Iridaceae Family; also Iris virginica.

Habitat: Grows in moist meadows and on the borders of swamps. While known to grow in the wet soil of eastern North America, it may be found in other areas where the growth need requirements are met.

Growth needs: Wet moist soil, with fair amount of sunshine.

Description: Pale bluish-green leaves mark the Iris versicolor while bright green leaves are typical of the Iris virginica. The latter has lilac colored flowers while the former has violet-blue flowers.

Parts used: Stem and root.

Effects: This herb has a cathartic (cleansing) and diuretic (kidney stimulating) effect. It stimulates the cleansing of the body and the result is a feeling of relaxation.

Recorded uses: This herb has a record of a multitude of uses. By boiling an ounce of the root powder or root itself in water (pint), it is said to increase the flow of urine and thus aid in elimination of poisons from the blood; also, the drink is said to aid in the colic (pains in abdominal area due to gas) and is also reported to relieve cases of whitish discharges from female genital passages. It has also been recommended for relieving coughs and for headaches. Inhaling some of the powder induces sneezing, helping to clear the nasal passages. The juice of the root is reported to ease the

pain of piles or hemorrhoids. The root powder is reported
to cleanse and heal wounds, even deep ulcers. It has been
used as folk medicine in the past for blood impurities, liver
diseases, skin diseases, syphilis and rheumatism. It is also
a mild laxative and has been used for dropsy, an abnormal
and excessive accumulation of matter in various glands of
the body. It is also recommended for non-malignant enlargement of lymphatic and thyroid glands. The headache
and dizziness of indigestion are also relieved with this herb.
When made into an alcoholic tincture, with one ounce of
the powder to a pint of pure alcohol, the dosage should be
from ten to twenty-five drops in water three times a day.
One-half cup of water should be adequate.

For use as a cathartic (to cleanse intestines) the dosage
of the root powder should be twenty grains. (For compari-
son purposes, the average pill or tablet, in compressed form,
weighs about seven grains.) For ordinary use, not requiring
any drastic action or stimulation, a dosage of about ten
grains has been found to be sufficient.

Prior to modern use of penicillin and other wonder
drugs, Blue Flag was widely used for its curative value in
venereal infections such as syphilis. Doctors may eventually
return to the use of Blue Flag as the body tends to fail to
respond to certain so-called wonder drugs, due to repeated
use. Probably many doctors have continued to use Blue Flag.

A small dose of the tincture, perhaps ten drops to one-
half cup of water, has been found helpful for headaches in
the right supraorbital region of the head (over the right
eye) when accompanied by nausea and vomiting. This type
of headache is believed to be the result of liver disease.

Several authorities recommend Blue Flag as a vermifuge to rid the body of worms that sometimes become lodged in the intestines.

Blue Flag has also been reported to have been used as a remedy for bites and stings of insects or other poisonous creatures. An ounce of the powdered root would be boiled in water (a pint) with about a tablespoonful of vinegar. An average dose would be one-half cup every hour of this mixture until the symptoms disappear.

BLUE MALLOW

Also known as Common Mallow, Mauls.

Botanical name: Malva sylvestris.

Effects and reported uses: The entire plant, including the flowers, has beneficial value. The dried plant is allowed to dry and then ground into powder form. If desired, the whole dried plant may be crumpled and placed into a container instead of the powder, but when this is done it is more difficult to measure the correct amount of herb in relation to the water. This herb has both internal and external uses reported. A pint of boiling water is poured over about one-half ounce of the herb and then allowed to stand for a few minutes until the water has cooled to drinking temperature. Drinking this infusion has been found to be a popular cure for coughs, colds and similar ailments. A teaspoonful of the powder may be taken as a dose two or three times a day in lieu of preparation of the drink, or the powder may

be obtained in tablet form or placed into gelatin capsules
and the capsule then dissolves in the stomach. The herb
itself, preferably in powder form, may be applied directly
to various body parts and the effect is to soothe the part
or soften the skin to which the herb is applied. It is a sticky
or mucilaginous substance, and it has no odor.

BOLDO

**Also known as Boldu, Boldea
fragrans.**

Botanical name: Peumus Boldus.

Effects and reported uses: The leaves of this herb, im-
ported from Chile, serve as a diuretic, stimulating secretion
and excretion of urine and also as a liver stimulant, being
useful in chronic liver or hepatic torpor (inactivity of the
liver) problems. It is also an antiseptic in that it prevents the
growth of micro-organisms, and this herb has been found
valuable in cases of inflammation of the bladder and for
destruction of gonorrhea germs in the urinary tract. The
dosage ranges reportedly from fifteen to sixty grains, with
smaller dosages for mild cases, and larger doses for aggra-
vated cases.

BONESET

**Also known as Indian Sage,
Thoroughwort.**

Botanical name: Eupatorium perfoliatum.

Effects and reported uses: One of the effects of this herb is to produce perspiration, and it is therefore called a diaphoretic. It is also a tonic because it strengthens tissue and it is a febrifuge because it lessens fever. It is an expectorant because it facilitates the removal of secretions of the mucous membrane of the bronchial tubes and it also has a mild laxative effect. It has been termed "a certain remedy in all cases of fever and influenza." It is also effective for catarrh or severe spells of coughing usually associated with asthma and emphysema. Another use of this herb is for various skin diseases. To prepare a drink of this herb, pour a pint of boiling water over an ounce of the powdered herb and allow to steep for about five or ten minutes. It will be effective whether taken as a hot or as a cold drink, one-half cup at a time several times a day. As a rule, it should be taken while hot for colds and to produce perspiration. When taken as a strengthening tonic, it may be taken cold. The dry powder may be swallowed as a dose, ranging from twelve to twenty grains in a dose. As a skin ointment, the powder may be mixed in equal proportions with vaseline to form a salve. In some cases, more effective results may be obtained by taking the powder and mixing it with sufficient water to make a clay-like preparation that may be applied directly to the affected part.

BORAGE

Also known as Burrage.

Botanical name: Borago officinalis.

Effects and reported uses: This herb is a diuretic, increasing action of the kidneys and the flow of urine. It is also a demulcent, softening the mucous membrane or skin to which it is applied. It has been successfully used for fevers and pulmonary (lung) complaints. A pint of boiling water is poured over an ounce of the leaves and the solution is allowed to steep for about ten minutes. One-half cup at a time may be taken several times a day. For external use, it may be used as a poultice to reduce inflamed areas or swellings, applying the leaves themselves for this purpose.

BOX LEAVES

Botanical name: Buxus sempervirens.

Effects and reported uses: This herb seems to be effective in purifying the blood and is recommended as a good tonic for debility or general weakness and especially liver jaundice, the disease marked by yellow skin due to changes in the liver cells causing the bile pigment to be diffused into the blood. The usual dosage is from twenty to sixty grains of the powdered herb, which may be taken as a tea or swallowed directly for quick absorption.

BRYONY

Also known as **Black Bryony**
and as **Blackeye Root.** Also, as
Bryonia.

Botanical name: Tamus communis, Linn. Family: Dioscoreacae.

Habitat: Europe.

Growth needs: Temperate climate, ample water and sun. Fairly good soil.

Description: Climbing vine with shiny heart-shaped leaves. Berries are egg-shaped and of deep red color. Flowers are green with six petals. The root is nearly cylindrical, about one to one and one-half inches in diameter. Rootlets are wire-like and blackish brown externally and white internally.

Part used: Root.

Effects: Brings blood to the skin; also, acts on kidneys to stimulate secretion of urine.

Recorded uses: Because one of the effects of this herb is to bring fresh blood to the part where the herb reaches, this herb has been successfully used by taking the fresh root, scraping it, and rubbing the pulp into parts affected by gout, rheumatism or paralysis. It is also recommended for removing discoloration due to bruises, accounting for the name "Blackeye Root." An ounce of the root mixed with a pint of pure alcohol will make a tincture of the root. One to five drops of the tincture has been found to be a sufficient dosage for internal use twice a day in some water or fruit juice to bring about additional flow of urine.

This herb has also been used for dropsy, the name for diseases where there is an accumulation of fluid in body

cavities or tissues. A few drops of the tincture in water (not
over five drops to a glass of water at a time) has been found
to be sufficient for results. Externally applied, the powdered
root, mixed with water into a paste and applied to the skin,
has been used to remove freckles and to help heal sunburns.
It has also been reported as effective in cleansing open ulcers
located on the surface skin of the body.

BUCHU

Also known as Thumb, Dios-
ma Betulina, Barosma Betulina,
Bookoo.

Botanical name: Rutaceae.

Habitat: South Africa.

Growth needs: Warm climate, rich soil.

Description: The plants are low shrubs with angular
branches and small leaves, growing opposite to each other
on the branches. The flowers range from pink to white in
color.

Part used: The dried leaf.

Effects: Causes a sense of heat in the stomach and then
this feeling gradually spreads throughout the body. The
pulse rate is increased, the appetite is stimulated and a slight

moisture of the skin is produced. The flow of urine is increased. If taken in large doses, it causes vomiting and difficulty in urinating. There is also a burning sensation in the stomach when a large dose is taken.

Reported preparation: An infusion (soaking the powdered leaf in hot water without boiling) is an effective means of preparation of this herb. About thirty grains of the powder (two grams) is reported sufficient for an average dose.

Recorded uses: Valuable for chronic diseases of the genito-urinary mucous membrane, such as in cases of cystitis, pyelitis, urethritis and prostatitis. This is also valuable in cases involving gravel stones in the urinary passages (lithiasis) as well as chronic bronchitis. It has also been successfully used in chronic rheumatism, affections of the skin, indigestion (dyspepsia) and in cases of accumulations of fluid in body cavities or in the cellular tissues (dropsy). This herb is also recommended for diabetes in the early stages. It has also been reported as valuable for cases of green-whitish discharge (leucorrhea) from the female vaginal passage.

NOTE: This herb has also been prepared in tincture form, mixing the buchu with pure alcohol in sufficient quantity to tint the alcohol. A dosage of ten to twenty drops in a glass of water has been used for results. Buchu may also be used as a tea for treatment of the diseases mentioned.

BUGLE

**Also known as Bugula, Common
Bugle.**

Botanical name: Ajuga reptans.

Effects and reported uses: This is an herb tonic for stimulating the tone of gastrointestinal mucous membrane. It
is also an astringent, as it checks secretions of mucous membrane tissue and contracts and hardens tissues. It has an
agreeable odor and so is an aromatic. It has been reported
widely used in cases where it is necessary to stop bleeding
(hemorrhages) and is known to be a remedy for disorders
of the bile. The method of preparing the drink is to pour
a pint of boiling water over an ounce of the herb and to
allow the solution to steep for about ten minutes. One-half
cup may be taken three or four times daily.

BUGLEWEED

**Also known as Sweet Bugle,
Water Bugle, Gipsywort.**

Botanical name: Lycopus Virginicus.

Effects and reported uses: This herb is a sedative, relax-
ing the nerves. It also has as astringent effect, tending to
contract tissues of the mucous membrane and to reduce

discharges of fluid. This herb is also a mild narcotic. It is used for coughs, and also for relief of bleeding from the lungs as consumption (tuberculosis). A drink is prepared by pouring a pint of boiling water over an ounce of the powdered bark. A cup at a time may be taken several times a day.

BURDOCK

Also known as Lappa, Lappa Minor, Hill, Thorny Burr, Lappa Major, Lappa Tomentosa, Burdock Root, Beggar's Buttons, Hareburr, Clot-bur, Bardana.

Botanical name: Lappa Arctium, Arctium Lappa, Arctium minus, Family Compositae.

Habitat: Europe, Asia and North America.

Growth needs: Has been found in waste places and along roads, indicating little need for any special soils, temperature, sun or water. This plant would therefore grow well if cultivated with some care so as to provide good soil, sun and water.

Description: The first year's growth consists of a rosette of rough, heart-shaped or oblong type leaves with solid, deeply furrowed stalks. The stem rises to as high as nine feet in the second year. The leaves are irregular toothed and

there are clusters of purple tubular flowers. The fruit is
oblong, flattened and angular. It does not open and contains
a single seed, part of the fruit.

Parts used: The dried first year root and the seed.

Effects: Promotes flow of secretions of body without irritating qualities. Also, has a gentle laxative effect and stimulates action of the stomach.

Recorded uses: By pouring cold water on ground or
bruised dry roots of the herb, with a ratio of one ounce of
ground root to a pint of water, a decoction can be made
that is reported effective for such conditions as rheumatism,
gout, pulmonary (affecting the lungs) conditions such as
dischages from the lungs or air tracts to the nose. This herb
is also a mild laxative. In preparing the decoction, about
one-half pint of additional water should be added to make
up for the amount of water that boils away. An average dose
would be from a tablespoonful to a cupful, taken twice daily.

Drinking of this decoction has also been recommended
for chronic skin irritations. It has also been praised in relieving such conditions as tuberculosis of glands and bones
and abscesses resulting from this disease. The solution has
also been used effectively as an external application to relieve swellings, hemorrhoids and chronic sores.

The seeds of this herb have been successfully used in a
tincture to relieve severe and chronic skin conditions known
as psoriasis inveterata, recognized by scaly red patches on
the skin. The seed tincture has also been found helpful in
strengthening and improving the tissues of the stomach and
is recognized as a stomachic tonic.

Burdock is also known to be effective in stimulating flow of urine and also increases perspiration. It is considered as a blood purifier, tending to restore abnormal conditions to normalcy. An outstanding characteristic of Burdock is the ability of this herb to reach the glands of the body and to cleanse and normalize the inner membrane of the glands.

As Burdock contains volatile oils, which evaporate rapidly at ordinary temperature when exposed to the air, it is desirable to prevent the loss of the oil in the herb by dissolving the herb in alcohol. The proportion is usually one or two ounces of the herb to a pint of alcohol. Alcohol also dissolves the gummy and resinous matter in the Burdock, including resin and tannin. The usual reported dosage is from ten to twenty-five drops of the tincture in water, three to four times a day.

BUTTERBUR

Also known as Common Butter-bur.

Botanical names: Petasites vulgaris, Tussilago, Petasites.

Effects and reported uses: This herb has several valuable effects. First, it is a cardiac tonic, strengthening the heart muscles. It is also a stimulant, temporarily increasing functional activity of organs, and it is a diuretic, increasing functional activity of the kidneys. It has been successfully used as a remedy in fevers, asthma, colds and urinary complaints. It relieves cases of gravel or stones in the bladder

and is generally considered suitable for widespread contagious disease. The root of this herb is boiled for about fifteen
minutes in the proportion of one ounce to a pint of water.
The solution is taken frequently about one-half cup at a
time, three or four times a day.

CALOTROPIS

Also known as Mudar Bark.

Botanical names: Calotropis procera, Asclepias procera.

Effects and reported uses: When taken internally, the
bark of this particular tree has been found beneficial for
diarrhea and for dysentery, the condition of inflammation
of the intestinal tract. The powder is applied directly to the
skin for chronic cases of skin disease (eczema), skin leprosy
and elephantiasis, a chronic skin affection with excessive
growth of cellular tissues. The dosage for internal use is from
three to twelve grains three times a day. When applied directly to the skin, the bark should be in powdered form in
solution with water, olive oil or antiseptic vaseline. This
herb is popular in India where elephantiasis, a tropical disease, is prevalent. This disease is caused by worms infesting
the lymphatic circulation.

CAMPHOR

**Also known as Gum Camphor,
Laurel Camphor.**

Botanical names: Cinnamomum Camphora, Laurus Camphora, Camphora officinarum.

Effects and reported uses: Camphor is obtained from large trees in Formosa by passing steam through the chipped wood. The distillate contains camphor, which is separated and again heated until evaporation, to obtain oil of camphor. Taken internally, it is valuable in colds, chills and in diarrhea associated with colds. It acts as a sedative, quieting the nerves. It also is a pain remover, and is valuable for spasms such as those associated with asthma. It increases perspiration and at the same time reduces fever. It has also been used to expel intestinal worms. It is reported as beneficial for cases of gout, rheumatism and neuralgia, the disease marked by severe, piercing pains along the course of a nerve, usually due to faulty nerve nutrition. Camphor is also highly valued in cases of irritation of the sexual organs. Externally, camphor can be safely applied in all cases of inflammation, bruises, sprains and similar ailments. Excessively large doses for internal use should be carefully avoided, to avoid vomiting, convulsions and an abnormally rapid heart beat. Physicians will sometimes use oil of camphor as a cardiac (heart) stimulant. An average dose for internal use should not exceed three grains.

CAROBA

Also known as Carob Tree, Caaroba.

Botanical names: Jacaranda procera, Jacaranda Caroba, Bignonia Caroba.

Effects and reported uses: This is an herb that alters the processes of nutrition and excretion, restoring the normal functions of the system. It has been successfully used in the venereal disorders, especially in syphilitic skin affections. It also has a soothing or sedative effect upon the nervous system and it has also been reportedly effective in cases of epilepsy. One of the effects of this herb is to increase perspiration, and it also increases activity of the kidneys, increasing production of urine.

CASCARA SAGRADA

Also known as Purschiana bark, Persian bark, Sacred Bark, Chittam bark, Bearberry, Chittem Wood bark, Dogwood bark, Coffee-berry bark, Pigeonberry bark, Bitter bark, Rhamnus Purshiana, Bear Wood, California Buckthorn.

Botanical name: Rhamnus Purshiana, Family Rhamnaceae.

Habitat: Southwestern Canada, Washington, Oregon and northern California.

Growth needs: Rich soil, sun and ample water.

Description: The bark is taken from a small tree reaching a maximum height of approximately twenty feet. Its leaves are rather thin with an oblong shape, rounded edges (elliptic), and with the leaf edges being of a saw-like (serrated) nature. The fruit is black, three-lobed and three-sided.

Parts used: The bark.

Effects: The fresh bark contains a principle which acts as a gastro-intestinal irritant and emetic. The bark is usually stored for at least a year before being used, to reduce the powerful effect.

Recorded uses: Successfully used for chronic constipation without forming a habit. Highly rated as a tonic for the intestines and recommended as a remedy for gallstones. It is said to increase the secretion of bile and is good for liver complaints, especially cases of enlarged liver. Four teaspoons of the powdered bark in a quart of boiling water, allowed to steep for one hour, produces a valuable drink. One or two cups a day, one hour before meals or on an empty stomach, is sufficient for good results. This herb is also obtainable in tablet form for ready use when needed. The tablets may be taken immediately after meals or upon retiring.

Another use for this herb is reported, in connection with chronic gout. It is also used for cases of gas in the stomach (dyspepsia) and in the treatment of piles, in producing large, soft and painless evacuations. The bowels are reported as acting naturally and regularly after use of this herb.

CASTOR OIL PLANT

Also known as Castor Oil Bush,
Palma Christi.

Botanical name: Ricinus communis.

Effects and reported uses: This is the well-known and popular cathartic and purgative that does so well in evacuation of the bowel. It has a mild action and so is highly recommended for young children and child-bearing women. It is usually taken in fresh or warm milk to disguise the oily taste. In addition to cases of constipation, it is also valuable in cases of colic, marked by cold extremities and hard and distended abdomens in infants. It is also valuable in cases of diarrhea resulting from slow digestion and after some herb has been administered to destroy worms, castor oil will help to remove them from the intestinal tract. Castor oil may be applied externally for itches, ringworm and cutaneous complaints. The dose varies from one teaspoonful for the very young to four teaspoonfuls for adults. In some areas, native women have used the fresh leaves of the castor oil plant as a poultice for application to the breasts to increase milk secretion.

CATECHU, BLACK

Also known as Cutch.

Botanical names: Acacia catechu, Catechu Nigrum, Uncaria Gambier.

Effects and reported uses: This herb is an astringent and is therefore useful for arresting excessive mucous discharges and for checking bleeding. It is also used in cases of chronic diarrhea, chronic catarrh and chronic dysentery, all diseases involving mucous membrane. The dose is from five to fifteen grains of the powdered leaves and young shoots of this herb. It is also recommended as a direct local application for spongy gums. A teaspoonful of the herb mixed with a pint of warm water has been found to make an effective gargle for sore throat.

CATNIP

Also known as Catmint.

Botanical name: Nepeta Cataria.

Effects and reported uses: This herb removes gases from the intestinal tract. The dosage is two tablespoonfuls of an infusion produced by pouring a pint of boiling water over an ounce of the leaves of the herb. For children, the dosage is smaller, perhaps two or three teaspoonfuls, which may be taken frequently to relieve pain in the abdominal area. An enema of the liquid may also be given to reach the large intestine. Another effect of this herb is to produce perspiration, and for this reason it is very useful in colds and similar ailments. It is a tonic, strengthening the tissue, and is a refrigerant, relieving thirst and reducing fever.

CAYENNE

**Also known as African Pepper,
Guinea Pepper, Bird Pepper,
Chillies.**

Botanical names: Capsicum minimum, Capsicum fasti-
giatum.

Effects and reported uses: This herb is said to be the
purest and most certain stimulant, producing a natural
warmth and improving circulation. It has been highly recommended for persons subject to exposure to cold and
damp, and the taking of this herb is said to be able to ward
off diseases caused by exposure. It has also been highly recommended in cases of ordinary colds by a dosage of from
five to twenty grains of the herb in warm water.

CELERY

**Also known as Smallage, Celery
Fruit, Celery Seed.**

Botanical name: Apium graveolens, Family of Umbelliferae.

Habitat: Originally in Southern Europe but now grown
in the United States. Main supply of celery is now grown
in Michigan and Wisconsin.

Growth needs: Good soil, sunshine and ample water supply.

Description: Grows every other year (biennial) and sometimes annually. The mature leaves are from six to fifteen inches long. The stem has three pairs of leaves and a terminal leaflet at the end of the stem. The fruit is brown and roundish.

Parts used: The dried ripe fruit and the seeds.

Effects: Tonic and stimulant.

Recorded uses: This herb has been highly recommended for rheumatism and also for excess gas in the stomach (flatulence). It is also known as a stimulant for the kidneys, inducing increased flow of urine. The tonic and stimulant effect is also known to stimulate the sexual appetite, as an aphrodisiac. Celery is popular as a flavoring. There are several ways of absorbing the beneficial ingredients. The oil in the seeds may be extracted by compression or the seeds (approximately an ounce) may be placed in a cup and hot water poured on them or on the dried ripe fruit and allowed to steep for one-half hour. The liquid is then strained out and dosages of one or two tablespoonfuls at a time will be sufficient for good results. The dosage may be repeated every four hours until results are obtained. When the oil of the seeds is used, two drops are sufficient for a dose.

The celery stalks are a popular food. The skin of the stalk is usually removed before the stalk is eaten. The skin is usually removed by blanching, that is, the stalk is dipped into scalding water and the skin then removed.

There are also some reports of benefits from partaking of celery in connection with liver problems or swellings in body cavities.

CHAMOMILE

Also known as Roman Chamomile, Double Chamomile.

Botanical name: Anthemis nobilis.

Effects and reported uses: The flowers and leaves of this herb are dried and powdered and an ounce of the powder is used with one pint of boiling water to obtain a solution that excites action of the stomach. The dose should not exceed one-half cup and usually one or two doses are sufficient to obtain the desired results. This herb is also well known as a remedy for nervous conditions of women and it is also used to stimulate the menstrual function. The flower of this plant has been often used to form a poultice for relieving pain, by external application to the area. The lotion may also be used for toothache, earache and various other nerve pains by direct application to the part affected. The solution is also a tonic, having the effect of strengthening tissues.

CHAPARRAL

Also known as Encinilla.

Botanical names: Croton corymbulosus, Larrea Divaricata.

Effects and reported uses: Little has been known of this herb in the past except that the flowering tops, when boiled in water, have made a very palatable drink among Indians and early settlers of the southwest United States. It is still regarded by many as a good coffee substitute. Recently, the chaparral tea has had some promising reports in cancer treatment, according to studies made at Utah University and the University of Nevada, Reno.

CHAULMOOGRA

Also known as Chaulmugra, Chaulmogra, Chaulmoogra Oil.

Botanical name: Taraktogenos Kurzii. Another plant, Chaulmoogra odorata, has, in the past, been confused with this herb but the seeds of that plant are quite different.

Effects and reported uses: There are three ways of administering this herb. The seeds may be powdered and given in doses of from three to six grains at a time. Oil may be expressed from the seeds and applied as an ointment with a base of a substance such as petrolatum, and a third method is to administer the oil internally, mixed with almonds or milk to suit the taste. When taken internally, this will produce a sedative effect and it lessens fever. When applied externally, it relieves stiffness of joints and eruptions of the skin such as eczema and psoriasis. It has long been used for skin eruptions resulting from tuberculosis, syphilis and rheumatism.

CHERRYLAUREL

Botanical name: Prunus Laurocerasus.

Effects and reported uses: The leaves of this herb are reduced to powder and the dosage is from fifteen to sixty grains, depending upon the age of the individual. Children should be given smaller doses. It has a sedative effect and relaxes the muscles involved in coughing. It has been found valuable, therefore, in attacking coughs, including whooping cough. It is also of value in asthma, resulting from affections of the bronchial tubes. It has also been reported to be of value in cases of stomach gas or indigestion.

CINNAMON

Botanical name: Cinnamomum Zeylanicum.

Effects and reported uses: Cinnamon is a bark, usually sold in powdered form, that has several effects and uses. It is an astringent, tending to contract tissues and to reduce discharge. It is aromatic, having a pleasant fragrance. It is stimulating to body organs and it is a carminative, that is, it removes gases from the intestinal tract. It is especially useful for weakness of the stomach and for diarrhea and it has the effect of checking nausea and vomiting. It is often combined with other remedies. Dosage is from fifteen to sixty grains at a time, taken twice daily.

CLEAVERS

Also known as Clivers, Goose-
grass, Hayriffe, Erriffe, Bur-
weed, Goosebill, Goose grass,
Gravel grass, Grip grass,
Goose's hair, Clabber grass,
Catchweed, Savoyan, Milk
sweet, Poor Robin, Bed-
straw, Scratchweed, Cleaver-
wort, Cheese rent herb, Aperine,
Goose-share.

Botanical name: Galium aparine of the Family Rubi-
aceae.

Habitat: England.

Growth needs: Hardy plant. Grows along edge of roads.
Needs little cultivation.

Description: The plant will grow six to nine feet high
and may climb trees if the plant contacts a tree. The stalks,
leaves and seeds are so rough that they will cleave to almost
anything they touch. Small white flowers bloom each year,
but the roots die. New plants start from fallen seed. The
leaves are about one-half inch long and one-quarter inch
broad, shaped like the point of a lance (lanceolate). The
leaves have bristly hairs at the margins and the fruit is
nearly globular, about one-eighth inch in diameter, covered
with hooked bristles.

Part used: Entire plant, including seeds.

Effects: Produces perspiration (diaphoretic) where desirable, such as in fevers where a free outward circulation is desirable; relieves irritation; mild laxative; relieves inflammations of kidneys and bladder; stops bleeding from wounds; helps functions of the liver; cleanses the blood.

Recorded uses: In addition to the uses indicated above, this herb makes an excellent wash for the face to clear the complexion. The herb has the quality of cooling or refrigerating the skin, thus being valuable in fever cases where it is desired to reduce the temperature. The juice of the leaves, applied to a bleeding wound, stops the bleeding. The powder of the dried root, sprinkled on wounds, will tend to hasten healing, and similar sprinkling on open ulcers has resulted in quick formation of healing coverings. The juice of the herb has been used to stop earaches, by dropping some of the oil into the ear. Hot water poured on the dried herb makes an infusion. The liquid is then strained away and is then suitable for drinking. This herb is reputed to dissolve bladder stones. Use one ounce of the herb to a pint of hot water.

CLOVES

**Also known as Clavos, Caryo-
phyllus.**

Botanical name: Eugenia aromatica of the family Myrtaceae.

Habitat: Molucca Islands of Indonesia. They are also cultivated in Ceylon and the islands of Zanzibar and Pemba.

Growth needs: Hot tropical climate.

Description: The clove trees are evergreen and reach a height of thirty or forty feet. The leaves have a leathery texture (coriaceous) and are covered with many depressions.

Parts used: Unexpanded flower buds.

Effects: The aromatic oils of cloves have a stimulant an irritant effect. The blood circulation is increased and the temperature is slightly raised. The digestion of food is improved and the food values are better utilized. Pain and spasms are relieved due to the anesthetic effect of the oils, which are excreted from the body through the kidneys, skin, liver and the bronchial mucous membrane. The oils stimulate and disinfect as they travel through the bodily organisms.

Recorded uses: Used to promote the flow of saliva and gastric juices; to relieve pain in the stomach and bowels; to correct conditions of gas in the stomach; to correct the gripping tendency of many purgatives and to flavor pharmaceutical preparations. Applied externally, cloves relieve the pain in chronic rheumatism, lumbago and toothache. This herb also relieves the pain of muscle cramps and some nerve conditions (neuralgia), the oil of cloves being applied along the course of the nerve. The average dosage for internal use, in powdered form, is from two to five grains. For toothache, one or two drops on the tooth will usually stop the ache. Cloves may be prepared as a tea, with a cup of boiling water poured over a teaspoonful of the clove powder and allowed to steep for a few minutes. Such a drink has been used to relieve nausea (dizziness) and vomiting.

COFFEE

Also known as caffea.

Botanical name: Coffea arabica.

Effects and uses: This plant, or rather, its seeds, have stimulant, anti-narcotic and anti-emetic effects. As a stimulant, the caffeine in the coffee seeds or beans stimulates the heart. It is anti-narcotic in that the coffee will help dispel stupor and drowsiness resulting from poisoning by narcotics and it will serve as a remedy for headaches in many cases. It also serves as an anti-emetic by acting to prevent vomiting. When taken in excess, it may produce unpleasant heart symptoms. It has been often used to dispel the effects of excessive alcohol and coffee has a decided diuretic effect, causing increased activity of the kidneys. It has been reported to help those affected by gout, rheumatism and gravel stones in the bladder.

COHOSH, BLACK

Also known as Black Snakeroot, Rattleroot, Rattleweed, Squaw-root.

Botanical names: Cimicifuga racemosa, Actaea race-mosa, Macrotys actaeoides.

Effects and reported uses: The root of this herb is an astringent, contracting tissues and tending to reduce dis-charges of body fluids. It is also a diuretic, tending to activate functions of the kidneys, and it is an alterative, restoring the normal functions of the system in the processes of nutrition and excretion. It is useful in diarrhea of chil-dren in small quantities such as a dose of not to exceed three grains. For adults, a dosage of five or six grains is adequate. This herb also stimulates the menstrual flow and it is especially valuable in cases of coughing, reducing the rapidity of the pulse and inducing perspiration and is very beneficial in cases of whooping cough. It is frequently used as a remedy for rheumatism and is said to be specifically appropriate for cases of children having involuntary, jerk-ing motions, a nervous disease known as chorea and also as St. Vitus' Dance.

COMFREY

Also known as Gum plant, Heal-ing Herb, Knitback, Slippery Root, Nipbone, Knitbone, Con-solidae, Blackwort, Rus-sian Comfrey, Comfrey Root, Common Comfrey.

Botanical name: Symphytum officinale of the Family Boraginaceae.

Foreign names: French, Consoude; German, Beinwurz or Schwarzwurz.

Habitat: Originally introduced from Russia into England. It now grows extensively throughout Europe, Canada and the United States.

Growth needs: Needs to be well watered, with a fair amount of sunshine. Good soil needed.

Description: This is a perennial herb growing up to three feet in height, with a thick, spindle-shaped (fusiform) root, tapering from the middle toward each end. The leaves are large and hairy, either green or dark yellow, with pointed ends.

Parts used: Root and leaves.

Recorded uses: This herb is probably used for more different purposes than any other herb. Reported uses are as follows:

PULMONARY DISEASES: For diseases of the lungs, including pneumonia or coughs, an ounce of the powdered root or leaves is placed in a container, over which is poured a pint of hot water. The mixture is then stirred and allowed to soak for about fifteen minutes. One-half cup of this infusion may then be taken four times a day.

SCROFULAR DISEASES: These diseases usually involve enlargement and degeneration of the lymphatic glands, often resulting in tumors and ulcers. The aforementioned infusion may be taken for relief of these conditions. In addition to the glands, the skin and mucous membrane may also become enlarged and may be helped by this herb's action.

DIARRHEA: The infusion aforementioned has also been found to be helpful in relieving cases of diarrhea, as well as in relieving inflammation of the membrane of the large intestine, referred to as dysentery.

LEUCORRHEA: This is a condition of excessive secretions from the mucous membrane of the female genital organs, and reports indicate that this herb, taken as an infusion as outlined above, will relieve this condition.

CALCIUM DEFICIENCY: This herb has been reported as being very rich in easily assimilated organic calcium.

COLDS AND COUGHS: The infusion aforementioned, taken hot, has been found to be of value in the relief of colds and coughs.

SORES: Sores or ulcers on the outside of the body have been relieved by preparing a poultice made of the crushed green leaves or of the powder of either the leaves or the root.

STOMACH CONDITIONS: Various stomach conditions, including cases of stomach ulcers, have been aided by this herb. The leaf or root powder is usually placed in the small gelatin capsules (size 0) and two or three capsules taken before meals for several days.

ARTHRITIS: To provide relief from the pains of arthritis, this herb may be used by applying a hot compress or poultice of the herb, either crushed green leaves or moistened powdered herb (leaf or root), to the painful part.

GALL AND LIVER CONDITIONS: Reports indicate that comfrey, in the form of an infusion, will relieve gall and liver conditions. It has been reported that gall stones (solid substances found in the gall-bladder) are so affected by comfrey as to relieve this ailment.

ASTHMA: Although a difficult ailment to correct, comfrey has been reported to relieve asthma conditions, when it is taken in a hot drink as described above.

TONSILS: There are reports that comfrey poultices of powdered herb, applied about the throat, will relieve acute cases of ulcerated tonsils with high temperature present.

GENERAL CLEANSER: Comfrey is recognized as providing a general cleansing action throughout the entire system of the body tending to establish a normal condition.

GASTRIC AND DUODENAL ULCERS: In addition to aiding stomach ulcers, this herb is reported as being of value in ulcers involving the small intestines, known as the duodenum. The powder, taken in gelatin capsules, will usually relieve any pains in the stomach, a condition known as gastralgia.

PRURITUS ANI: This is a condition of itching in the region of the anus or rectum. The direct application of the powdered leaf or root will usually result in a healing of the tissue.

CUTS AND WOUNDS: Unless a wound is severe, the direct application of the powdered leaf or root will result in the formation of a scab immediately, and healing of the injury will usually take place much more rapidly than ordinarily. In any severe wound, a physician should be called to stitch the parts together. However, there are cases when comfrey has been used in severe wounds penetrating to the bones with good results, due to the ability of this herb to draw the parts together. Many years ago, before X-rays were used to determine the precise position of fractured bones, comfrey was widely used to bring fractured bones together.

TRAUMATIC EYE INJURIES: The application of a poultice of comfrey to the area of the eye is recommended by herbalists for relief of the pain and for remedial care of the bruised area.

HEADACHES: A poultice of this herb is also recommended for headache pains occurring in the lower back part of the head, the top of the head and the forehead.

BREASTS: In cases of swollen breasts due to excess milk, the application of a poultice of comfrey is reported to be very beneficial.

HEMORRHOIDS: Application of the powdered leaf or root will repress bleeding of hemorrhoids.

GOUT: Comfrey is also recommended for the gout, a poultice being made of the comfrey root powder and placed over the area of pain.

GANGRENE: In cases where a body part has become gangrenous, the use of comfrey poultices has been found in many cases to be helpful.

BURNS: In addition to the many other good qualities of comfrey, it has also been found valuable in cases of burns. The comfrey forms a protective coating and helps the body in the formation of new skin.

NUTRITIVE: As comfrey contains a large percentage of protein, it may be regarded as a nutritive food. When fresh comfrey leaves are liquidized in a base of some fruit juice, such as unsweetened pineapple juice, the result is a nutritious drink that has been known to relieve many ailments. In some instances, other herbs have been added to the drink, such as alfalfa, parsley, dandelion, mint, kale or other healthy food.

KIDNEY STONES: Reports have been published of comfrey, taken in the form of a tea infusion, curing cases of kidney stones.

ANEMIA: Comfrey has been found valuable for cases of anemia, increasing appetite and providing nutrients needed by the body. It may be taken with unsweetened pineapple juice or as a tea. It may also be swallowed in the form of gelatin capsules.

BLOODY URINE: One author has referred to comfrey as the "best remedy for bloody urine." The comfrey may be taken in several forms, but for this type of complaint the concentrated form, in gelatin capsules, would probably be most effective.

TUBERCULOSIS: Comfrey has been recommended for tuberculosis, as apparently there are elements in the comfrey that enclose and inactivate the area of the disease.

FEMALE DEBILITY: Another herbalist refers to comfrey as being valuable for cases of weakness of women, especially where women have been unable to bear children or have otherwise lost their vigor and have too little sexual desires.

SKIN PROTECTION: Combining comfrey with a good face or hand lotion produces a product that has been found valuable for removing various imperfections on the skin. Where wrinkles are due to lack of nutritive elements in the skin, the composition of comfrey is such that wrinkles will tend to disappear. However, there can be no assurance that comfrey will always remove wrinkles in all types of skin conditions.

COTTON ROOT

Botanical name: Gossypium herbaceum.

Effects and reported uses: The bark of the root of this herb affects the organs of reproduction. It is reported to contract the uterus and is used in cases of difficult and obstructed menstruation to stimulate the menstrual function. The herb is reputed to be useful in removing sexual lassitude or weariness. Two ounces of the powdered bark of the root is used. A pint of boiling water is poured over the herb and the solution is allowed to stand for a few minutes. It should be used while freshly made. This may be taken several times a day. It is also reported to be used to hasten or bring on childbirth sooner.

COUCHGRASS

Also known as Twitchgrass, Quickgrass.

Botanical names: Agropyrum repens, Triticum repens.

Effects and reported uses: The root of this herb is excellent for bladder and urinary complaints and it stimulates activity of the kidneys and increases the flow of urine. It is soothing and softening to the mucous membrane and is also recommended for the gout and rheumatism. It is also a mild purgative. To prepare the solution, pour a pint of boiling water over an ounce of the powdered herb.

CULVER'S ROOT

Also known as Leptandra, Culver's Physic, Tall Speedwell, Veronica, Bowman's Root, Tall Veronica, Black Root.

Botanical name: Veronicastrum virginicum; veronica virginica; leptandra virginica; of the Family Scrophulariceae.

Habitat: Found in low grounds of Canada and United States as far south as Alabama and west to Minnesota and Nebraska.

Growth needs: Grows best in the mountain meadows of the south and the rich woods of the north. Requires ample water supply and rich soil, with shade.

Description: A tall plant from three to eight feet high, it flowers in July and August. The flowers are small, pinkish to nearly white and arranged in spikes with flowers in clusters. The leaves are in whorls of four or seven.

Parts used: Roots and rhizomes. (Rhizome is the stem between the root and the point where branches start.)

Effects: Strong laxative effect, with a special effect on the liver. In large doses, it will produce vomiting. It also tends to increase flow of bile.

Recorded uses: For relief of indigestion in the duodenal area (first portion of the small intestine). It has also been recommended for use in chronic indigestion where there are insufficient secretions from the bile. The dried root is less active as a laxative but, when fresh, the root has a strong and violent cleansing action upon the intestines. This herb is also regarded as a tonic. This herb is known as a cholagogue, meaning that it produces a flow of bile. The liver normally produces a pint or more of bile every twenty-four

hours. Bile is a strongly alkaline substance (fluid) functioning to neutralize the acid which enters the intestines from
the stomach. This herb stimulates the liver to produce more
bile.

DAMIANA

Also known as Turnera, Dami-
ana Leaves.

Botanical name: Turnera aphrodisiaca, of the family
Turneraceae. Another botanical name is Turnera diffusa.

Habitat: California, Mexico, West Indies and South
America.

Growth needs: Warm climate, large amount of sunshine,
ample water, good soil.

Description: This herb grows as a shrub or small tree.
It is regarded as tropical and requires a warm climate. The
stalks are short and the leaves are narrow and pointed.
Reddish-brown twigs are intermixed with the leaves. Flowers are yellowish. The taste is bitter with a fig-like flavor.

Parts used: The dried leaf.

Effects: Damiana is widely known as an aphrodisiac
and as a tonic for the nerves.

Recorded uses: An old remedy for sexual impotence (aphrodisiac). It is reputed to greatly strengthen the reproductive organs. The herb also has a mild laxative effect and mildly stimulates the kidneys to increase the flow of urine. There are also reports of use in cases of exhaustion of a mental as well as of a muscular nature. It is known as a tonic for the nervous system, and has been reported useful in sick headaches, and in some cases of mild paralysis.

A quick and inexpensive method of preparation is to take approximately a teaspoonful of the macerated dried leaves or one-quarter teaspoonful of the ground leaf powder and to pour a cup of water (boiling) upon the herb. Dosage would be about a tablespoonful twice daily.

DANDELION

Also known as Taraxacum, Lion's Tooth, Swine Snout, Puff Ball, Wild Endive, Priest's Crown, White Endive, Blow Ball, Cankerwort, Dandelion Root.

Botanical name: Taraxacum officinale, of the Family Compositae.

Habitat: Europe and North America.

Growth needs: Thrives in any good soil. Cultivation is necessary to keep down weeds. The roots of wild plants should be dug either in the early spring or in the fall.

Description: The underground root is long and tapering and branches at the top into two or more branches or crowns. From the roots, bright-green, saw-toothed leaves, with the teeth inclined backward, grow in rosette-formed shapes. Later, a hollow stem rises from the center of the rosette, bearing a broad orange-yellow head of strap-shaped flowers. The fruit is greenish-brown, containing one seed, and with a slender stalk crowned by a silky, spreading round head of fruit seeds.

Parts used: The dried root or prostrate stem (rhizome) that produces roots below and leaves above. The entire green herb, including leaves, is also used.

Effects: Has the effect of a tonic and mild laxative.

Recorded uses: It is chiefly used in kidney and liver disorders. An old popular way of using this herb is to allow the roots to dry, roast them in the oven, then grind and use as coffee is ordinarily used, allowing it to percolate or to steep in boiling hot water for about fifteen minutes. It is a tonic and a moderate purgative. It also acts as a diuretic to stimulate the flow of urine. It also stimulates activity of the stomach and in addition to increasing activity of the liver, also stimulates the pancreas and spleen. It is also reported to have a beneficial effect on the female organs and is reported beneficial for skin diseases, scurvy (resulting from Vitamin C deficiency), tuberculosis diseases of lymphatic glands, diabetes and cases of inflammation of the bowels or accumulation of fluid in body tissues or cavities. Eaten green, it serves as an excellent fresh green salad, containing natural nutritive salts that purify the blood and destroy the acids in the blood. This relieves anemic conditions. As a cold drink, a cup is filled with the green leaves and boiling water added and steeped for about thirty minutes, or a teaspoonful of the powdered root may be used instead. Drink when cold three times a day.

DIGITALIS

Also known as Foxglove, Figwort, Purple Foxglove, Digitalis folium P.I., Folk's-Glove, Fairy's-Glove, Ladies' Glove, Dead Men's Bells, Digitalis Leaves, Digitalis Leaf, Foxglove Leaves, Fairy Cap, Fairy Fingers, Fairy Thimbles, Fairy Bells, Flopdock, Throatwort, Cottagers.

Botanical name: Digitalis Pulverata and Digitalis Purpurea. Part of the Figwort Family known as Scrophularia-ceas.

Habitat: Grows throughout Europe in meadows and pastures. It is now grown in various parts of the United States both as an ornamental flower for the garden and for its medicinal value. It is under cultivation in New York, Oregon and Washington as well as in the New England states.

Growth needs: Grows on dry sandy ground with a minimum of care. While water and sun are always welcome to plants, only a small amount is required for this plant.

Description: Tall plant with alternate leaves with long purple or white flowers. Its leaves have a velvety surface with short hairs. The flowers are tubular-shaped with white spots.

Parts used: Leaves.

Effects: Gives rest and tone to heart muscle and stimulates kidney action.

Recorded uses: This herb has a long record of use as a heart stimulant and tonic. It has also been found to act to reduce swollen organs of the body, or rather, the cellular tissues of the body. It was long the common practice to take about one-eighth ounce of the dried powdered leaves and pour a pint of boiling water over it and allow to steep for about one-half hour. Doses are from a teaspoonful to a tablespoonful. This herb has now been widely adapted by the medical profession and there has been considerable experience obtained from its use. A danger in the use of Digitalis is that it may over-stimulate the heart muscle and ultimately cause a paralysis of the heart. In some instances, such as aortic constriction, Digitalis is contra-indicated. Consequently, Digitalis must be used with the greatest care, and under a doctor's direction.

ECHINACEA

**Also known as Black Sampson,
Coneflower, Pale Purple Cone-
flower, Nigger-head, Kansas
Nigger-head, Red Sun-flower,
Purple Coneflower.**

Botanical name: Echinacea Angustifolia; Brauneria pallida; Rudbeckia pallida; Brauneria Angustifolia; Echinacea
Purpurea.

Habitat: Found in the prairies west of the Mississippi
River; some varieties have been reported growing in Vir-
ginia and westward to Illinois and southward to Louisiana.
Generally, it is found in the Central United States.

Growth needs: Moderately rich and well-drained loam
(mixture of sand, clay and organic matter). Plants should
be left in the seed-bed for two years before transplanting
to the field.

Description: This plant is a shrub with a stout stem
arising to the height of three feet or less. The leaves are
narrow and the purple flowers are cone-shaped. Rhizome
and roots are cylindrical or slightly tapering.

Parts used: Rhizomes (growth between root and leaves)
and roots.

Effects: Antiseptic qualities destroying bacteria and blood cleanser.

Recorded uses: Blood impurity diseases such as boils, gangrenous conditions, bites and stings of insects, spiders or snakes, pus formations, sores, infections, wounds, sore throat (used as gargle), tonsilitis, typhoid fever, abscesses, glandular inflammations, cerebro-spinal meningitis, diphtheria, tetanus, septemia (infection of blood), uremia (condition of blood containing urea, ordinarily excreted as urine through the kidneys) and ulcers. It is reported to have given relief in cases of dyspepsia (difficult and painful digestion) and relieves ulcer pain of the gastro-intestinal tract. This herb is reported as not having any toxic or other undesirable effects and is easily eliminated. Other reports indicate that this herb is also valuable in relieving diseases following childbirth. It has also been reported as having the power to stimulate sexual activity (aphrodisiac) and to have pain-ending (analgesic) powers. It has also been used to relieve hemorrhoids.

Preparation: Fifteen grains of the powder, twice daily, taken with water or fruit juice. Mix with water, for gargle use.

ERGOT

Also known as Ergot of Rye,
Smut of Rye, Spurred Rye.

Botanical names: Claviceps purpurea, Secale cornulum.

Effects and reported uses: This fungus obtained from grains of rye has been widely used in menstrual disorders of women such as leucorrhea (whitish discharge from the vagina and uterine cavity), dysmenorrhea (painful menstruation) and amenorrhea (absence or abnormal stoppage of menstruation). It is known to be an effective emmenagogue, promoting the menstrual flow. Another use for this product is for stopping the flow of blood, as in the case of internal hemorrhage or other internal bleeding such as intestinal bleeding. It is also of value in male disorders such as enlarged prostate, the gland surrounding the neck of the bladder and urethra in the male and in cases of spermatorrhea (involuntary discharge of semen) and the venereal disease gonorrhea. Dosage reported to vary from ten to thirty drops of the fluid extract of this herb.

EUCALYPTUS

Also known as Blue Gum Tree.

Botanical name: Eucalyptus globulus.

Effects and reported uses: The leaves of this tree and the oil distilled from the leaves have several beneficial medicinal effects. First, there is the antiseptic value. Although extremely potent as an antiseptic, its use is generally safe. It may be inhaled freely for sore throat and other bacterial infections of the bronchial tubes or lungs. It has also been found valuable for relief of asthma, when this is due to spasm of the bronchial tubes or swelling or inflammation of the mucous membranes of the throat or pulmonary

passages. A second use for this herb is as a local application
for ulcers and cancerous growths. Usually ulcers are healed
by preparing an application of one ounce of the powdered
leaves to a pint of lukewarm water, applied directly to the
parts in need of treatment. When oil is extracted from the
leaves, the oil may be used both internally and externally.
For internal use, a dosage of from three to ten drops is sufficient for good results. A third use for the oil is in cases of
fevers and in conditions of muscular spasms. A unique fea-
ture of this herb is that it causes offensive odors to cease
almost immediately. This is valuable in cases of sores or
other open wounds. A fourth use of the herb is in cases of
croup and spasmodic throat troubles and there may be both
internal and external uses of the oil or fluid extract. Great
care must be taken not to take excessive amounts of the oil
internally as large doses may produce indigestion, diarrhea,
nausea, vomiting, muscular weakness and other severe effects.

EYEBRIGHT

Botanical name: Euphrasia officinalis.

Effects and uses: A teaspoonful of one-half of the fluid
extract of this herb combined with an equal amount of the
fluid extract of Golden Seal has been found to be an excellent lotion for general irritating disorders of the eyes. The
herb has a slightly tonic effect and it is also an astringent,
drawing the tissues together and halting discharges.

FIG. 115

FIG

Also known as Fici, Ficus Caricae.

Botanical name: Ficus Carica, of the Family Moracae.

Habitat: Asia, Italy, Spain, Greece, California.

Growth needs: Hot sun, good soil and ample water supply.

Description: A small tree with spreading branches and grayish or red bark, the leaves being green and growing in an alternate manner. The leaves are palm-shaped and have from three to five lobes. The under side is hairy. The fruit is a pear-shaped, hollow, fleshy receptacle.

Parts used: The fruit and the leaves.

Effects: Nutritious, laxative and demulcent (soothing to irritated surfaces).

Recorded uses: Excellent as a nutritious food, containing dextrose (grape-sugar) for energy (62 percent), fat, proteins, starch and other vitamin and mineral elements. Other uses are listed below:

FOR BOILS: Split open the fresh, ripe fruit and lay on boil.

CONSTIPATION: Figs are mildly laxative and will help for relief in constipation.

WARTS: Before the fruit is ripe, when it is broken from the branch, a milk escapes that may be dropped upon warts and allowed to soak for several hours before ultimate removal.

SORES: The milk aforementioned may be placed upon sores to help in their healing. A tea made from the fig leaves may be used to wash the sores. Also, bathing sore spots due to bruises or blows with warm fig leaf teas will remove the discoloration and aid in the circulation.

NOSE AND THROAT: For nose and throat conditions, such as sore throat or asthma, the tea may be sniffed into the nose. When the tea is lukewarm, several drops may be dropped into the ear for pain in the ear. The tea is made by taking one heaping teaspoonful of finely cut leaves to a cup of boiling water.

COUGHS, ASTHMA and BRONCHITIS: Take a pound of figs, cut them up, bring to boil in a quart of water and allow to simmer for a few minutes. Place in cheese cloth and squeeze out the juice, adding the juice of two lemons. This is reputed to be excellent for coughs or for the various lung diseases.

FIGWORT

Also known as Rosenoble, Throatwort, Carpenter's Square, Scrofula Plant.

Botanical name: Scrophularia nodosa.

Effects and reported uses: This herb has great value in helping to heal all skin eruptions, wounds and abscesses. It has a decided cleansing effect and removes pain. The most effective method of application is to take the leaves and apply them as a poultice directly to the part affected. It may be taken internally as a diuretic, hastening the activity of the kidneys and promoting the flow of urine. A pint of boiling water poured over an ounce of the herb will produce a healing tea. Usually one-quarter cup of the drink has been stated to be sufficient, and may be taken twice daily.

FIREWEED

Botanical name: Erechtites hieracifolia.

Effects and reported uses: This plant has a wide variety of reported uses. It is known as an astringent, tending to reduce discharges and drawing tissues together. It is also pain-relieving and produces warmth. It is applied externally in cases of hemorrhoids, a condition where a mass of blood vessels have formed a tumor in the rectal mucous membrane area. The oil squeezed from this herb is used for this purpose. The oil, being anti-spasmodic in effect, is also recommended for spasms such as occur in colic (characterized in the infant by a distended abdomen) and in hiccoughs. The oil may be taken for internal use by placing five or ten drops of the oil in some sugar, to make it easier for small children to swallow. Adults may take the oil in gelatin capsules or may swallow the dosage in a small quantity of warm water. The oil may be also applied directly to relieve pain in cases of rheumatism, sciatic nerve conditions and in cases of the gout.

FLUELLIN

Botanical name: Linaria Elatine.

Effects and reported uses: This herb is an astringent, consolidating and strengthening tissues, and is highly recommended for internal bleeding, including bleeding of the nose and excessive bleeding during menstruation. One ounce to a pint of boiling water allowed to steep for a few minutes will produce a beneficial drink. One-half cup every two hours until relief is obtained is considered an average dose. For wounds on the outside of the body, there may be a direct application of the solution to the parts affected.

GARLIC

Botanical name: Allium sativum.

Effects and reported uses: The use of garlic increases perspiration and also serves as a diuretic, increasing functions of the kidneys and the flow of urine. It is also an expectorant, tending to remove mucus from the throat and lungs. The dose is usually from ten to thirty drops squeezed from the garlic bulb. It is also used to advantage in coughs, colds and asthma by making a garlic syrup, mixing a teaspoon of the garlic juice with some honey or sugar for ease of swallowing.

GELSEMIUM

Also known as Yellow Jasmine, Wild Woodbine.

Botanical names: Gelsemium nitidum, Gelsemium sempervirens.

Effects and reported uses: This herb, particularly its root, is valuable as a sedative and has been used successfully in insomnia or other conditions where a sedative is needed. It relaxes the nervous system, particularly the nerves in the arterial blood vessels. It is also a diaphoretic, increasing perspiration, and it is a febrifuge, reducing fever. It has also proved to be valuable in relieving the pains of toothache and neuralgia, the condition of severe, piercing pains along the course of a nerve. Very little of this herb is needed for effect. The ordinary dose is from one-half to two grains of the powdered root. It may be added that this herb has also been found useful in cases of inflammation of the bowels, a basic cause of diarrhea and dysentery.

GENTIAN

Also known as Gentian Root,
Bitter Root, Yellow Gentian
Root, Felwort, Baldmoney, Field
Gentian.

Botanical name: Gentiana lutea of the Gentianaceae
Family.

Habitat: Mountainous regions of central and southern
Europe.

Growth needs: Grows best in rich soil, with ample
water and sunshine.

Description: This herb grows to a height of about thirty
inches. The stem above the ground is thick and hollow. The
leaves are egg-shaped and fairly large, growing opposite to
each other on the stem. The flowers are orange-yellow. The
fruit is an ovate capsule and contains winged seeds.

Parts used: The dried root and the rhizome.

Effects: Tonic effect on tissues; also reduces feverish
conditions.

Recorded uses: A small amount of the powdered root
or the stem above the root (the rhizome), equal to two
tablets or about fifteen grains, serves as a valuable stomach

tonic, and as a tonic for the nerves. In addition to aiding the organs of digestion, this herb has also been recommended in cases of general debility, female weakness and hysteria. It has also been mentioned as valuable as a counter-poison, helping in cases of bites by poisonous "beasts."

GINGER

Botanical name: Zingiber officinale.

Effects and reported uses: The root of the ginger plant is a stimulant, tending to excite the glands to action, and it is also an expectorant, tending to loosen mucus in the throat and bronchial tubes. It also removes gases from the stomach and intestinal tract. It is widely used for colds and for stomach gas conditions. It may be taken as a tea with ten to twenty grains of the powdered ginger root in warm water. It is more palatable when sweetened.

GINSENG

Also known as Five Fingers Root, American Ginseng, Ninsin, Red Berry, Garantogen, Sang.

Botanical name: Panax quinquefolia, of the Family Araliacea.

Habitat: Mountains of eastern Asia and in Korea and Japan. It is also found in the eastern part of North America in the woodlands. Some roots grow in North Carolina, Kentucky and several other states.

Growth needs: Grows best in rich soil, with partial shade. Should be watered regularly.

Description: The stems of this plant are more or less hollow between the nodes of the stem and are solid at the nodes. The leaves alternate rather than growing opposite to each other on the stem. The root often roughly resembles the figure of a man, with legs, body and head.

Part used: The dried root.

Effects: Stimulates perspiration and normalizes the nutritive system.

Recorded uses: This herb has been used for loss of appetite, stomach and digestive affections arising from mental and nervous exhaustion and to stimulate perspiration. It will also stimulate other secretory glands, secreting products of the glands, such as the salivary glands. It is this characteristic of ginseng that has helped establish it as an aphrodisiac.

EYESIGHT: Ginseng has been recommended for eyesight difficulties where objects appear double and where there is difficulty in opening of the eyelids. It is also reported helpful for gray spots before the eyes, usually accompanied by dizziness.

HEADACHES: Ginseng has been recommended for headaches in the lower back part of the head as well as for semi-lateral headaches, partly to the side of the head.

BACK PAINS: Ginseng has been recommended for pain in the small of the back, in the thighs or for any stiffness of joints of lower limbs or stiffness of the back. It is reported as giving relief in cases of lumbago, sciatica and rheumatism.

MISCELLANEOUS: Reported good for paralytic weakness, hiccoughs and pimples.

GOA

Also known as Araroba, Bahia Powder, Brazil Powder, Ringworm Powder, Chrysarobine.

Botanical name: Andira Araroba.

Effects and reported uses: This powder, derived from a yellowish powder found in the trunk of the Goa tree, is valuable for destroying the taenia tapeworm, but it is more widely known for the treatment of skin diseases, such as eczema, psoriasis, acne and related skin diseases. For skin treatments, the powder is mixed with vinegar, lemon juice or glycerine for the formation of a paste which is then applied to the skin. When taken internally for tapeworm, the average dosage is reported to be from three to five grains of the powder in a teaspoon of honey.

GOAT'S RUE

Botanical name: Galega officinalis.

Effects and reported uses: A dosage of from five to twenty grains of the powdered herb has been found valuable for promoting the flow of milk of the nursing mother. It is also recognized as a diuretic, increasing kidney activity and the flow of urine, and is a vermifuge, destroying worms in the intestinal tract.

GOLDEN SEAL

Also known as Orange Root, Yellow Root, Hydrastis, Yellow Puccoon, Hydrastidis rhizoma, Ground Raspberry, Indian Paint. The French name is Sceau d'Or and the German name is Canadische Gelbwurzel.

Habitat: It is found in the rich, well-drained woodlands of North America, east of the Mississippi River. Plants are also cultivated in the Pacific northwest and in North Carolina.

Growth needs: This herb grows plentifully in the virgin forests of the United States. However, it has become very scarce as a wild plant in the past few years. These plants need to be planted in well-fertilized soil containing abundant leaf mold. It must be protected during the summer period against excessive light and heat. Vines are good protection for this purpose, and planting in lath houses is also satisfactory. The ideal location is on the sloping side of a woodland hill where the shade is abundant and the drainage is good.

Description: This herb consists of three parts, the aerial section above ground, the roots below the ground and the stem just below the surface, called the rhizome. The dried rhizome and the roots are the parts used. The portion above ground is only about six inches high and consists of one main leaf and two smaller leaves with five or seven lobes. There is a crimson red berry appearing somewhat like that of the raspberry. The roots are long and slender.

Physiological effect: This herb has the effect of constricting or tightening the blood vessels of the body. This is known medically as a vasoconstrictor effect.

Reported uses: Generally, in conditions where blood vessels need attention.

It is helpful as a general bitter tonic to rehabilitate conditions of mucous membranes, especially for gastric (stomach) disturbances where there are inflammatory conditions.

For cases of difficult and painful digestion (dyspepsia).

In the treatment of catarrhal conditions of the mucous membranes. (A condition of running secretions.)

In nose bleeds or other cases of passive hemorrhages or bleeding, such as bleeding from the pelvic tissues.

As an eye cleansing preparation and in the treatment of eye conditions where there is a running of secretions.

While used mainly for the effect upon the mucous membrane, this herb influences favorably all parts of the body. It is known to improve the appetite and to assist digestion and has been found valuable in cases of stomach ulcers and in general aid to the nervous system.

The tonic effect of this herb is of healing value to the liver and the system (portal system) of collecting blood from various parts of the body and returning the blood to the heart and lungs.

By combining with some bicarbonate of soda, this herb is excellent as a mouthwash and for relief of sores in the mouth and of the gums.

It has been recommended for favorable action on both the secreting and excreting functions of the liver.

It has been recognized as a superior aid for sore throat and eruptive sores.

It has also been used by doctors for ulcers of the vagina and uterus, as well as for eczema and smallpox.

All kinds of discharges from the genital organs are referred to as leucorrhea, for which this herb in tincture form, as well as taken internally, is recommended.

HARTSTONGUE

Botanical names: Scolopendrium vulgare, Asplenium Scolopendrium, Phyllitis Scolopendrium.

Effects and reported uses: This herb is specially recommended for removing various obstructions from the liver and spleen and for removing gravelly deposits from the bladder. It also has a mild laxative effect and it is effective in relieving chest conditions such as coughs. A pint of boiling water is poured over two ounces of the powdered herb and allowed to steep for a few minutes. The dose is one-half cup of the drink taken two or three times daily.

HAWTHORN

Also known as English Hawthorn, Hawthorn Berries, May, May Blossom, Whitethorn, Haw.

Botanical name: Crataegus Oxycantha of the family Rosaceae. This herb has also been classified in the family Pomacae.

Habitat: Originally grew throughout England in all counties, used as hedges, but also growing wild in waste ground and untilled places. It has been introduced into various parts of the United States on a small scale.

Growth needs: This is a hardy shrub that requires only a relatively small amount of water and sun. Soil need not be rich.

Description: Considered as either a shrub or a tree, depending on whether allowed to grow singly or in a group. The fruit is a small berry. Flowers are cup-shaped with five parts. Stems are thorny. The berry fruit is similar to apple or quince.

Part used: Fruit.

Effects: Tonic for the heart muscle. Dissolves crusty matter in arteries.

Recorded uses: Good results have been reported in connection with heart disease such as angina pectoris, heart valve defects, rapid and feeble heart action or hypertrophy (excessive enlargement) of heart. This herb has also been used in connection with dyspnoea or difficult breathing due to ineffective heart action and consequent lack of oxygen in the blood. It has been found that this herb is effective for removal of crusty matter in blood vessels, a disease known as arteriosclerosis, a thickening or hardening of the walls of arteries. The reported dosage is from three to fifteen grains of the powdered fruit three or four times a day. The powder may also be made into a tincture by taking a pint of grain alcohol and mixing an ounce of the powdered herb into it. From one to fifteen drops may be taken at a time, depending upon the condition and need for prompt action. Although mild and non-toxic, it may take several days or longer for good results to be obtained. A large dose may produce dizziness; therefore, dosage should be taken under a doctor's direction.

HEDGE MUSTARD

Botanical name: Sisymbrium officale.

Effects and reported uses: The dried herb in powdered form constitutes an excellent remedy for hoarseness and weak lungs. The average dosage is one-half to one teaspoon of the powdered herb in a pint of boiling water. A teaspoonful at a time may be taken every thirty minutes until the symptoms are diminished.

HELLEBORE, FALSE

Also known as Adonis, Pheasant's Eye.

Botanical name: Adonis vernalis.

Effects and reported uses: This herb is highly recommended for heart disease as well as for kidney ailments. It is especially valuable in enlarged heart conditions as well as in heart strain. One-quarter ounce of the powdered herb in a pint of boiling water produces a solution that has been found to be of benefit for these conditions. Care should be taken not to take more than a tablespoonful every two to three hours. It is basically a tonic for the heart muscle, and should be taken under a doctor's direction.

HONEYSUCKLE

Also known as Dutch Honeysuckle.

Botanical name: Lonicera Caprifolium.

Effects and reported uses: This herb is successful in coping with disorders of the respiratory organs and in asthma. It facilitates expulsion of the mucus from the mucous membrane of the throat and lungs. It is also a mild laxative. Both the flowers and the leaves are used, the dried flowers being mixed with honey in the proportion of approximately five grains to a teaspoonful of honey and the leaves being placed in boiling water in the proportion of one ounce of the powder to a pint of water. The leaves also serve as a mild laxative and have been found valuable in relieving ailments of the liver and the spleen.

HOREHOUND

Also known as Hoarhound, White Hoarhound and Marrubium.

Botanical name: Marrubium vulgare. Family: Labiatae.

Habitat: Native in Europe and Central Asia but naturalized in United States.

Growth needs: Thrives best in a sunny location. Water is needed, but the water should drain easily from the soil, which may be sandy and need not be rich.

Description: The stem will grow to about thirty inches in height. It is called White Hoarhound or Horehound because of a white hair-like substance on the plant that is both fragrant and decorative. The flowers are small and white, in tubular form, and arranged in dense whorls. The leaves are round and branches are of a spreading variety.

Parts used: The dried leaves and flowering tops.

Effects: Effective in detaching tissue particles from membrane.

Recorded uses: This herb has been used for many years in coughs, colds, asthma, hoarseness and other affections of the lungs (pulmonary diseases). The customary mixture is to take four ounces of the herb and to simmer for ten minutes in two pints of water. It is usually sweetened with honey, in a quantity sufficient to suit the taste. The usual dosage is one-half cup every three hours. It is often taken hot for best results. It is also regarded as a slight laxative. One of the older herb manuals recommends this herb as a menstrual aid for "women to bring down their courses." It is also recommended by earlier authorities as a general anti-dote for poisons, including cases of stinging or biting by poisonous snakes. The leaves of the herb, mixed with honey, have also been recommended for cleansing of foul ulcers or to stop running or creeping sores. The juice of the herb, mixed with wine and honey, has been said to clear the eye-sight. The same solution, inhaled, is said to clean away yellow jaundice. It may be used for various skin diseases by external application in mixture with some vinegar.

NOTE: There is also a Black Horehound, known as Mar-rubium peregrinum or Marrubium nigrum. It is similar to Horehound, except the flowers are usually purplish instead of white. It serves as a stimulant and vermifuge and has also been recommended for suppressed or excessive menstruation.

HOUSELEEK

**Also known as Common House-
leek, Sengreen, Joubarbe des
toits.**

Botanical name: Sempervivum tectorum.

Effects and reported uses: The fresh leaves of this plant
are bruised and placed directly on burns, stings and other
affections of the skin, including warts and corns. The leaves
serve as an astringent, reducing discharge and drawing the
tissues together. The poultice also has a cooling effect on
inflamed areas.

HYSSOP

Botanical name: Hyssopus Officinalis of the Family
Labiatae.

Habitat: Various parts of Europe, including the middle
east.

Growth needs: This is a hardy plant requiring only a
moderate amount of water and sunshine. It grows best in
an alkaline soil.

Description: The stem is rather woody and the leaves are pointed, about one-half inch long as compared with one-eighth inch in width. The leaves are hairy on the edge or margin. The flowers are blue and in tufts.

Part used: The entire plant. However, the leaves are most commonly used.

Effects: Acts as a general cleanser of the body system.

Recorded uses: Hyssop has been the symbol of cleansing and purification from the earliest days. The Bible (John 19:28, 29) refers to the offering of hyssop to Jesus at the time of the crucifixion. It has been found that the mold of penicillin grows on the hyssop leaf. An infusion prepared by soaking an ounce of the herb in a pint of boiling water is the customary remedy for colds, coughs, pulmonary tuberculosis (of the lungs) or other lung conditions. It has also been recommended for asthma or for swellings in the area of the throat. It is also recorded as having been found valuable in treating cases of shortness of the breath. If taken with honey, it is reported to destroy worms found in the intestinal tract.

If taken with freshly picked figs, the combination of figs and hyssop is reported to cleanse the intestinal tract and to reduce the amount of lymphatic fluid from cavities or from tissues of the body.

An old herbal manual reports that hyssop restores the normal color to the body when the liver has been damaged and yellow jaundice occurs. It is also reported to help to correct abnormal conditions of the spleen, when hyssop is taken with figs. Another use for this herb is for use in the removal of bruises on the body, by boiling with wine and applying it to the bruised area in combination with warm water. It is also reported to be valuable in helping epileptics. The herb is also known to quickly heal cuts or wounds when the green herb is ground and applied to the cut or wound.

IPECAC

Also known as Ipecacuanha.

Botanical names: Psychotria Ipecacuanha, Cephaelis Ipecacuanha.

Effects and reported uses: The root of this herb, in solution, has been named as giving relief in cases of pyorrhea, the condition marked by a discharge of matter from the gums, inflammation of the tooth socket, shrinking of gums, loosening of teeth, infected gums and constitutional disturbances associated with this condition. A mouthwash and gargle can be prepared by pouring a pint of boiling water over an ounce of the powdered root and allowing the solution to cool down to body temperature. The mouth should be washed with the solution several times a day until the condition improves. Another effect of this herb, when taken internally, is to increase perspiration, by causing capillaries and other vessels to relax and dilate. It also acts effectively as an expectorant when taken internally, tending to loosen phlegm in the respiratory passages, and is thus recommended for coughs and colds. Internal use also helps cases of inflammation of intestinal mucous membrane accompanied by ulceration, fever and bloody evacuations, a condition referred to as dysentery. The dose for internal use is one-half teaspoonful of the solution described above for use as a mouthwash or gargle. Any larger quantity for internal use may cause vomiting.

JAMBUL

Also known as Jamboo, Java-Plum, Jambool, Jamun, Jambol Seeds.

Botanical name: Eugenia Jambolana of the Family Myrtaceae.

Habitat: India.

Growth needs: Moderate climate, fair amount of sun and water.

Description: The seeds, from a native tree of India, are blackish-brown, about one-quarter inch long and slightly less in diameter.

Parts used: The seeds are most commonly used; however, the bark of the tree is also used.

Effects: Astringent and diuretic.

Recorded uses: This herb has been recommended for the treatment of diabetes. After only a short period of time,

the amount of sugar present in the urine has been reported
to be reduced. It is usually taken with or after meals, in
water or in other liquids. The seed is ground and powdered
and the average dose is between five to thirty grains, depending upon the severity of the illness. The seed coverings
should be removed before the seed is ground and the seeds
should not be subjected to heat. There are two types of
diabetes, known as diabetes mellitus and diabetes insipidus.
While there can be no guarantee of cure, this herb has been
found useful in the treatment of diabetes mellitus. Symptoms of this disease are great thirst, weakness, emaciation
due to lack of insulin. When there is an excessive quantity
of sugar in the blood, the sugar finds its way into the kidneys and into the urine. In diabetes insipidus, the urine is
simply watery, without sugar.

JEWEL WEED

**Also known as Pale Touch-
me-not, Balsam Weed, Spotted
Touch-me-not, Speckled Jewels.**

Botanical names: Impatiens aurea, I. biflora.

Effects and reported uses: Jewel Weed has a mild purgative effect and also is a diuretic, increasing activity of the
kidneys. The fresh plants are boiled in lard to form an excellent ointment for hemorrhoids. The juice of the plant is
reported effective for removal of warts, corns and similar
growths on the skin. Also, it will relieve cases of ringworm
on the skin. It is also recommended for cases of jaundice

(liver ailment) and dropsy, the condition of morbid accumulation of water in the tissues and cavities of the body. For jaundice and dropsy, a drink is prepared by mixing an ounce of the powdered herb with a pint of boiling water. One-half cup of the solution is taken three or four times a day.

JOHN'S BREAD

Also known as St. John's Bread.

Botanical name: Ceratonia siliqua.

Effects and reported uses: The pods of this plant have sufficient nutrition to be used as a basic food for man. It is reportedly used by some singers to improve the quality of the voice.

JUNIPER BERRY

Also known as Horse Savin Berries.

Botanical name: Juniperus communis. Family Coniferae.

Habitat: Usually found in dry woods of the United States, Canada, Europe, Asia and Northern Africa.

Growth needs: Grows best in fairly rich soil in partially shaded areas such as forests. Needs only a small amount of water.

Description: This is a low evergreen tree or erect shrub, sometimes reaching a height of thirty feet. The leaves are thin, straight and long, needle shaped with sharp stiff points. The seed-bearing cones are egg shaped (ovoid) and each cone is divided into three fleshy scales (leaf-like), each scale containing one rudimentary seed which, upon fertilization, becomes a seed.

Parts used: The berries or fruits. (These are smooth and shiny, ranging from one-quarter inch to one-half inch in diameter and are purplish-black to dusky red purple.)

Effects: Stimulant effect on the body functions.

Recorded uses:

The berries are prepared as an infusion by first soaking several tablespoons of the berries, then adding them to a pint of boiling water for one-half hour or more. After cooling, the drink is divided into four portions and taken morning, noon, afternoon and evening. This infusion has long been a family remedy as a stimulant of the kidneys, usually taken when the kidneys do not function properly or when there is some irritation of the urinary passage.

NEURITIS: This herb is *not* to be used when there is any inflammation of the nerves, the condition known as neuritis.

DROPSY: This herb has been recommended for dropsy, a condition where there is an accumulation of fluids in various parts or cavities of the body. In such cases, small doses are advised.

INDIGESTION: This herb has been used with benefit as a stomach tonic and digestion aid.

GONORRHEA: This herb is also reported to be of value in cases of coping with gonorrhea.

LEUCORRHEA: This is a condition of a discharge of a greenish white mucus from the female genital passages, for which this herb has been found valuable. It should be used as a douche.

DISINFECTANT: The solution of this herb, while not harmful to the body unless taken in heavy dosages, is excellent for disinfecting a room by spraying it with the solution. It is believed to thoroughly destroy all bacteria and fungi. It is also valued as a gargle to disinfect the throat. The whole berries may be chewed as a means of disinfecting the mouth and throat.

APHRODISIAC: This herb increases or tends to increase sexual passion or power, stimulating the sexual appetite.

SCURVY: This condition is characterized by swollen, spongy and bleeding gums or bowels and by great weakness and occasional rheumatic pains. This usually results from the absence of fresh vegetables in the diet. This herb has been recognized as valuable to relieve this condition.

COUGHS: This herb is regarded helpful in easing coughs.

SHORTNESS OF BREATH: Juniper berries are reported as excellent for coping with shortness of breath.

SKIN DISEASES: Skin itches, scabs and even leprosy are reported to be aided by this herb. Bathing the skin with the Juniper solution has given reportedly beneficial results.

GOUT: This herb drink (infusion) is also reported to be good for the gout and conditions of inflammation of the fibers and ligaments of joints.

MISCELLANEOUS: Good results have also been reported for aiding conditions of sciatica, as well as generally strengthening of limbs of the body. It is also reported as beneficial for hemorrhoids, and drinking of the infusion is reported valuable for ridding the bowels of intestinal worms. The brain is also reported helped, memory is aided and the optic nerve is strengthened.

FLAVORING: The oil of the juniper berries is used to flavor gin and to impart to this drink the diuretic power (ability to increase activity of the kidneys) that is generally known to be associated with the drinking of gin.

THE PROSTATE: This herb is also reported to be valuable in treating diseases of the prostate gland, one of the symptoms of the disease of this gland being an excessive discharge of fluid. The discharge is usually of a slimy mucous nature.

NEPHRITIS: This is an inflammation of the kidneys and the use of this herb is *not* indicated when this condition is present.

CULINARY USES: Juniper berries are widely used when preparing game meat to remove the strong, gamy taste that is objectionable to many diners. Before roasting game, it is best to parboil the game in a good beef stock to which lemon, bay, leaves and juniper berries have been added. The berries also add a pleasing flavor to meat and game stews. The use of from four to six berries is usually sufficient.

JURUBEBA

Botanical name: Solanum Insidiosum.

Effects and reported uses: The root and fruit of this herb have been used with success in liver and spleen disorders as well as in cases of anemia and amenorrhea, the condition marked by absence of menstruation. The dose of the root in powdered form is from five to thirty grains in water.

KELP

Also known as Seaweed, Bladder-wrack, Sea Oak, Kelpware, Black Tany, Bladder Fucus, Seawrack.

Botanical name: Fucus vesiculosus, of the Family Fucaceae.

Habitat: This seaweed is found along coasts and borders of inlets of the North Atlantic and North Pacific Oceans between low and high tide marks. It is also found in various other parts of the world.

Description: This is a plant-body without a true root, stem or leaf. It grows near the surface of sea-water, attached to rocks or to mussels along banks by means of a series of expanded tendril tips which hold the plant fast. The color is dark brown and the plant has many forks or branches.

Parts used: Entire plant.

Effects: Remedial and normalizing action on organs, especially the thyroid.

Recorded uses: The high iodine content of this plant, providing an ample supply of iodine to the body, has made this plant valuable for cases of obesity, because of the normalizing effect upon the thyroid gland. Other recorded uses are:

REPRODUCTIVE ORGANS: This plant is reported to have a remedial and normalizing effect upon the reproductive organs, including the prostate gland, the uterus, the testes and the ovaries.

ARTERIES: It has been reported that kelp cleanses the arteries, removing deposits from their walls, thus restoring their elasticity.

SKIN: The presence of silicon in kelp is reported to keep the skin from wrinkling and sagging. Silicon is also an important food for the roots of the hair and an ample supply of kelp will usually prevent hair from falling out. The fingernails are also aided by the presence of kelp, which not only contains silicon but also calcium and sulphur, which are all needed for healthy fingernails.

INDIGESTION: The presence of sodium in kelp helps the digestive system to absorb food and also aids in preventing acidosis.

HEART: The manganese found in kelp is reported as being beneficial for tissues of the heart.

COLON: Kelp also has the effect of cleansing the colon, clearing away from the large intestine (the colon) many toxic substances that have adhered to the lining of the intestine and have been constantly absorbed into the blood stream, causing nervous disorders, rheumatism, kidney troubles and severe headaches.

ANEMIA: Kelp helps to relieve anemia, it is reported, due to the presence of iron and copper in kelp, which helps the body to obtain a sufficient supply of red corpuscles. Red corpuscles are essential in order for the blood to be able to absorb oxygen from the lungs. It is the lack of red corpuscles, therefore, that causes anemia.

BRAIN: Brain tissue is reported to be benefited by kelp because of the quantity of manganese in kelp, which is helpful to the brain tissue. Kelp is also reported as being of great value to the sensory nerves and to the meninges, the membrane surrounding the brain and spinal cord.

VITAMINS: Laboratory tests indicate that not only does kelp contain iodine and a number of important minerals, but it also contains Vitamin C, Vitamin A, many of the B-complex vitamins and Vitamin E.

KIDNEYS: Kelp is also known as a diuretic, stimulating the kidneys to eliminate waste water from the system. Kelp also protects the inside lining of the urinary passages.

DOSAGE: Usually one ten-grain tablet or two five-grain tablets per day is sufficient for good results. Another method of taking kelp is to take an ounce of the powdered kelp and pour a pint of boiling water over the powder and allow it to steep for about ten or fifteen minutes. A cup of this infusion twice a day is usually sufficient.

LARKSPUR

Also known as Lark's Claw, Lark's Heel, Knight's Spur.

Botanical name: Delphinium Consolida.

Effects and reported uses: A tincture of this herb is used to destroy parasites and insects as well as hair lice. Small doses may be taken internally for spasmodic asthma and for dropsy. A dose of ten drops is an average dose, the tincture being prepared by taking an ounce of the powdered herb and adding to it one pint of pure alcohol. It is allowed to stand for two weeks and the liquid then poured off and bottled for use. The medicinal power of the herb is absorbed, retained and preserved in the alcohol. The ten-drop dosage may be repeated several times a day until relief is obtained. For removal of hair lice, the hair should be washed thoroughly with the tincture.

LEMON

Also known as Limon.

Botanical names: Citrus Limonum.

Effects and reported uses: The juice of the lemon may be freely used as a tonic or as a remedy for colds. It is a refreshing drink in cases of fever, headache, pains or other symptoms of a cold. It is a popular remedy for coughs and colds. The juice of the lemon may be mixed with honey to make a healthful syrup.

LILY-OF-THE-VALLEY

Also known as Convallaria, May Lily.

Botanical name: Convallaria majalis.

Effects and reported uses: The effect of this herb is similar to that of Foxglove or Digitalis, but an advantage of this herb is that there is no danger of unpleasant disturbances. It is a tonic for the heart and has been used in many cases of heart disease, especially in diseases of the valves of the heart. The herb is also a diuretic, improving the function of the kidneys and increasing the flow of urine. Dosage is one tablespoonful taken two or three times daily. The preparation is prepared by pouring a pint of boiling water over one-half ounce of the herb powder.

LOBELIA

Also known as Indian Tobacco, Pukeweed, Wild Tobacco, Bladder Podded Lobelia, Asthma Weed, Emetic Weed, Gag Root, Eye Bright, Vomit Wort.

Botanical name: Lobelia inflata of the Lobeliaceae Family.

Habitat: United States, mostly from Massachusetts, New York and Michigan.

Growth needs: The soil should be rich loam. Seeds must be sown on the surface of the soil. Ample water is needed and a fairly large amount of sunshine.

Description: This herb has an erect, yellowish-green, branched stem reaching a height of approximately twenty inches. The leaves are round or oblong, growing in alternate positions on the stems. The cylindrical stem is sometimes purplish and has numerous hairs. The flowers are pale blue.

Parts used: Entire herb and seeds.

Effects: Tends to loosen mucous matter from mucous membranes; also a stimulant.

Recorded uses: The following is a summary of uses of this herb, as indicated in various reliable sources:

COUGHS: In coughs where there are accumulations of mucous, an infusion of a pint of boiling water to an ounce of the powdered herb, taken two tablespoonfuls every four hours, will usually relieve the cough. This is true in cases of croup, whooping cough, asthma, or bronchitis.

LIVER: The cleansing effect of this herb has been recommended and apparently used very successfully in various liver diseases, as this herb removes obstructions in the liver.

EMETIC: Where something is needed to induce vomiting, lobelia is highly recommended for this purpose.

ULCERS: By mixing with the herb Slippery Elm, this herb is recommended as a stimulating poultice for healing of inflammations, ulcers, swellings or similar conditions.

NERVOUSNESS: Lobelia is recommended as excellent for very nervous patients, as it is known to relieve brain tensions even where the patient is delirious. It may be combined with Pleurisy Root for relaxation of a disturbed patient.

FEVERS: Where there is a fever, this herb makes the pulse more full and soft.

HEART: For cases of angina pectoris (neuralgia of the heart), where there is pain in the heart region due to pressure on nerves of the heart, lobelia has been highly recommended for this condition.

LARYNGITIS: For both children and adults, this herb will relieve congestion of the mucous membranes and will usually give prompt relief in cases of laryngitis.

ASTHMA: Lobelia rapidly clears the air passages of the lungs of sticky or adhesive foreign matter.

VOMITING: When taken in large quantities, lobelia will induce vomiting; however, when taken in small doses, it will stop spasmodic vomiting.

INTERNAL BATHING: This herb may be administered by means of the internal bath, namely, taking a solution of one ounce of the powdered lobelia to a quart of water and injecting this solution into the intestines, through the rectum. The bowels are lined with tiny blood vessels which will absorb the herb into the system. This method of taking this herb (or other herbs) is sometimes desirable when the person being treated is a child and will not take any medicines or when an adult is so ill that the effort of sitting up and swallowing is too difficult or in the event there is immediate vomiting of anything taken by mouth.

LUCERNE

Also known as Alfalfa.

Botanical name: Medicago sativa.

Effects and reported uses: This plant is reportedly used for arthritis. The herb is reduced to powder and mixed with cider vinegar and honey, with one teaspoonful of each in water. This is considered a weight adding tonic and also strength-giving. Another method is to prepare a tea by placing about an ounce of the plant in a pan and pouring a pint of boiling water over it and allowing it to steep for several minutes before drinking.

LYCOPODIUM

Also known as Vegetable Sulphur, Common Club Moss, Wolf's Claws, Lamb's Tail, Fox Tail.

Botanical name: Lycopodium clavatum of the family of Lycopodiaceae.

Habitat: Europe and United States. Also Asia and Central America. In Europe, it is produced mainly in Poland, Switzerland, West and East Germany and the Ukraine. In the United States, much of it is produced in Maine.

Growth needs: This is a hardy plant requiring a minimum amount of good soil, sunshine and water.

Description: This plant grows close to the ground in a creeping fashion. The branches spread horizontally. The leaves are usually ranked in order and crowded. The leaves bear sporophylls or sacs of spores. (Spores are tiny reproductive bodies found in flowerless plants, which, after maturing, fall to the ground and divide and grow new plants.)

Part used: The spores. (Size of spore is 1/800th of an inch in diameter)

Effects: Long used as a protective dusting powder; facilitates healing.

Recorded uses: The spores contain about 47 percent of a bland, fixed oil, and it has been frequently used to relieve rheumatism and epilepsy. It has also been used in diseases of the lungs and of the kidneys. The oil in the spores results in the ground spores being valuable as a dusting powder over broken skin. As an internal remedy, the ground spores are mixed with milk-sugar (lactose) in the proportion of ten parts spore powder to ninety parts of lactose. A decoction is made by boiling approximately an ounce of the mixture with a pint of water for about fifteen minutes. A tablespoonful taken three times daily should suffice. It is also reported valuable for cases of stomach gas and constipation in addition to cases of congestion of the liver. Because of its tendency to assist in the healing of injured mucous membrane, this herb is useful in the healing of

aneurisms or swellings of arteries. It has been found valuable
in relieving itching of the anus (outlet of rectum).

MAPLE, RED

Also known as Swamp Maple.

Botanical Name: Acer rubrum.

Effects and reported uses: This is an astringent that has
been widely used by American Indians for sore eyes. It
strengthens the tissues and tends to eliminate discharges
of fluid.

MARIGOLD

Also known as Marygold, Garden Marigold, Calendula.

Botanical names: Calendula officinalis, caltha officinalis.

Effects and reported uses: This is a stimulant that is
used as a local remedy for direct application to varicose
veins, chronic ulcers and similar ailments. It increases perspiration and flushes poisons from the body. A solution for
both internal and external use is prepared by taking a pint
of boiling water and pouring it over an ounce of the powdered flowers and stems of the herb. By taking a dose of
one tablespoonful at a time two or three times a day, the
local action will be aided by the internal effects.

•   MASTERWORT

Botanical name: Imperatoria Ostruthium.

Effects and reported uses: This herb stimulates functional activities of various body organs. It is antispasmodic, tending to stop spasms, and it is also a carminative, removing gases from the gastro-intestinal tract. It is recommended for asthma, a disease characterized by spasms in the bronchial tubes, and it is also recommended for apoplexy, the disease of loss of consciousness and paralysis due to hemorrhage into the brain or spinal cord. It is also recommended for dyspepsia, a disease or condition of imperfect digestion. The root of this herb is used. An ounce of the powdered root is placed in a pint of boiling water and then allowed to steep for several minutes. Dosage is one-half cup taken two or three times daily.

MESCAL BUTTONS

**Also known as Muscal Buttons,
Pellote.**

Botanical names: Lopophora Lewinii, Anhalonium Lewinii.

Effects and reported uses: The fruit of this herb is of value as a heart or cardiac tonic such as in cases of angina pectoris, the heart condition of pain and oppression about the heart characterized by severe pain radiating from the heart to the shoulder, thence down the left arm. Dyspnea, a condition of labored or difficult breathing usually accompanied by pain, is also present frequently in angina pectoris. A pint of boiling water is poured over the dried fruit and allowed to stand for a few minutes. A tablespoonful of the liquid may then be taken every hour until the symptoms are relieved. An excessive amount of the herb may bring about vomiting. The herb is recognized as a narcotic and may bring about a stupor or sleep, or even complete unconsciousness.

MISTLETOE

Also known as European Mistletoe, Birdlime Mistletoe.

Botanical name: Viscum album, Phorandendron flavescens.

Effects and reported uses: The leaves of the plant have special value in cases of epilepsy (convulsions during unconsciousness), hysteria (nervous condition marked by alternate crying and laughing, usually during emotional stress), and other nervous conditions. This herb acts as a tonic and is also a narcotic, tending to induce a stupor, sleep or unconsciousness. It has also been recommended for female ailments, including hemorrhages of the uterus, amenorrhea (cessation of menstruation) and dysmenorrhea (painful or difficult menstruation). It has also been recommended as a heart tonic in cases of typhoid fever and has also been suggested for excessive or high blood pressure.

MUIRA-PUAMA

Botanical name: Liriosma ovata.

Effects and reported uses: The powdered root of this herb is a nerve stimulant especially recommended in cases where an increase in sexual desire is sought. As such, it is a well-known and popular aphrodisiac. A pint of boiling water is poured over an ounce of the powdered herb and allowed to steep for at least ten minutes. A small amount is sufficient for results, usually a dosage of from ten to sixty drops.

NIGHT-BLOOMING CEREUS

Also known as Sweetscented Cactus.

Botanical names: Cereus grandiflorus, Cactus grandiflorus.

Effects and reported uses: This herb has the effect of stimulating the heart to greater activity and reportedly gives prompt relief in most cardiac diseases such as heart palpitation (abnormally rapid throbbing or heart fluttering), angina pectoris (pain and oppression about the heart), cardiac neuralgia (nerve pains of the heart) and possibly other heart conditions. It has also been found of benefit in treatment of ailments of the prostate gland of the male, and gives relief in cases of irritated bladder and congested kidneys. It has also been recommended for women having headaches during their menstrual periods. This herb is a diuretic, aiding in the formation and flow of urine. The best formulation is to obtain the juice of the fresh plant, using the stem and flowers. The average dosage ranges from two to ten drops.

NUX VOMICA

Also known as Quaker Buttons, Poison Nut.

Botanical name: Strychnos Nux Vomica.

Effects and reported uses: The seeds of this herb are used as a tonic for general health, as a bitter, for stimulating the tone of the gastro-intestinal mucous membrane and as a general stimulant. It has been found valuable for coping with impotence (a weakness or inability to copulate), general debility or weak function of body organs and the nerve pains of neuralgia. It is also valuable in chronic constipation as it stimulates peristalsis or movement within the intestines. Only a slight amount is required for effective results as an excessively large dose could be poisonous. One to three drops of a fluid extract of the seeds is usually sufficient for satisfactory results. A pint of boiling water may be poured over an ounce of the seeds to produce the fluid extract.

OATS

Also known as Common Oats, Cultivated White Oats, Panicle Oats.

Botanical name: Avena sativa. Family Graminacae.

Habitat: Cultivated extensively in temperate zones of both hemispheres.

Growth needs: Thrives best in wet soil and a moderately cool, humid climate. The United States leads in the production of this grain.

Description: The whole oat is somewhat spindle-shaped, with the color a light yellowish-brown to a weak greenish-yellow. The grain is slightly over one-half inch in length. Whole oats are oats with the coverings or husks. Groats are oat kernels deprived of their husks. Oatmeal and Rolled Oats are prepared by removal of the husks and then rolled or ground. So-called "quick oats" are kernels that are first partially cooked before rolling in order to lessen the time required in preparing the product for food.

Effects: Nutrient and demulcent (soothing mucilaginous medicine).

Recorded uses: Used for indigestion and constipation by taking a tablespoonful of oatmeal and stirring it slowly in a pint of boiling water for about five minutes, adding a little salt to suit the taste. Some milk may be added if desired. One herbal recommends this drink for persons "who seek to retain their youth." The use of honey to sweeten the drink is permissible. The drink is recommended as a splendid tonic to the general system and is stated to be beneficial to the sexual system. Oats are composed of 67 percent carbohydrates, 14 percent albuminoids, amino-acids, enzymes (amylase, protease, lipase) phytin and vitamins A, B1, B2, E and traces of other vitamins. A poultice of oatmeal helps relieve itchy skin and ulcers and is reported to be used extensively in relieving sore conditions in the area of the anus and to dissolve hard formations. For nourishment for persons having difficulty in retaining food that is swallowed, oatmeal water, remaining after the oatmeal is strained out, may be used as a nourishing enema, after the rectum is first well cleaned and flushed. Oatmeal has many elements that have antiseptic properties, and when taken frequently as a food, is a natural preventative for contagious diseases. Another oatmeal drink, in addition to the drink previously mentioned, is to take a heaping tablespoonful of oatmeal and pour it into a quart of water and allow it to simmer for about two hours in a tightly covered pan. The oatmeal is strained out of the drink and the water is then cooled off in the refrigerator. Some honey may be added for sweetening, if desired.

FOR THE BRAIN AND NERVES: A most important use for oats is its use as a nerve tonic, as a restorative in nervous prostration and following exhaustion as the result of diseases accompanied by fever. The presence of phosphorus in oats makes this product valuable for the formation of brain and nerve tissue, and it was believed in bygone times that ample use of oatmeal will help children become more adept in their studies.

FOR THE HEART: An authoritative work on herbs states that oats "seem to exert a very beneficial action upon the heart muscles." The plentiful taking of oatmeal and/or oatmeal water has been considered as a preventative for heart disease as well as for helping to remedy heart disease.

FOR URINARY PROBLEMS: Oats have been recommended for relieving spasmodic conditions (involuntary contractions) of the bladder and ureter.

FOR INSOMNIA: Because of the beneficial effects upon the nervous system, the consumption of oats in the form of oatmeal or as a fluid extract has been reported to facilitate sleep.

FOR LOSS OF SEMINAL FLUID: One of the effects of oats is reported as beneficial in cases of involuntary loss of seminal fluid, known as spermatorrhea. Acting as a tonic and stimulant toward normalcy, oats strengthen the nerves and tend to promote normal nerve functions.

FOR FRECKLES AND OTHER SPOTS: It has been reported that boiling oats in vinegar and then applying the resulting oatmeal mash to the face or other parts of the body will remove the spots.

OLIVE

**Also known as Lucca Oil, Sweet
Oil, Salad Oil, Provence Oil,
Virgin Oil.**

Botanical name: Olea Europae.

Effects and reported uses: This is an often used remedy
for constipation and is popular as a laxative for children,
being often substituted for Castor Oil. Olive oil is helpful
in removing stony deposits from the bile and removes intestinal worms. The dose of the oil varies from one teaspoonful to a tablespoonful. It is used externally, either
alone or with other ingredients, as an ointment or a salve
for bruises, burns, scalds and various skin conditions. It is
also helpful in rheumatism conditions. It is valuable for rubbing gently on the gums of teething children and by absorption keeps the bowels regular.

ONION

Botanical name: Allium Cepa.

Effects and reported uses: One of the effects of the onion
is to act as a diuretic; that is, it serves to stimulate the action
of the kidneys and promotes the flow of urine. Roasted
onion is also used as a poultice for tumors or ulcers espe-

cially where there is pus formation. When placed against the ear, such a poultice is also good for earaches. Onion juice may be mixed with some honey and swallowed as a reputed cough cure. The boiled onion, when eaten, is helpful in relieving a cold.

PARAGUAY TEA

Also known as Mate, Yerba Mate, Jesuit's Tea, Brazil Tea.

Botanical name: Ilex Paraguayensis.

Effects and reported uses: The leaves of this tea have a diuretic effect, increasing action of the kidneys and the flow of urine. It is also a stimulant due to the presence of caffeine in the leaves. It is used in many areas of South America as a beverage instead of tea, coffee or cocoa. In large intake or doses, it acts as a purgative. It has been recommended for rheumatism and gout. It is prepared similarly to ordinary methods of tea preparation, with hot water poured over about a teaspoonful of the broken or powdered leaves in a cup.

PASSION FLOWER

Also known as Maypops, Passion Vine, Wild Passion Flower.

Botanical name: Passiflora incranata, of the Family Passifloraceae.

Habitat: West Indies and southern United States. It is now cultivated in many areas of the world, including Italy, Belgium and many other countries.

Growth needs: Ample sunshine, water and fairly good soil.

Description: This is a perennial climbing vine herb, continuing to grow throughout the year, with coils at the plant ends to enable it to climb. The flowers are large, solitary and whitish, with a triple purple and pink crown. The fruit is a round berry containing numerous round, flattened seeds that are covered with a yellowish or brownish accessory seed covering.

Parts used: The dried flowering and fruiting top.

Effects: Acts through brain and nervous system to relax tensions.

Recorded uses: The following is a summary of the reported uses:

SEDATIVE: It is considered a reliable remedy in treating nervous disorders, including insomnia, hysteria and other conditions. It is especially valuable during convalescence and during the menopause.

FEVERS: It is usually given in feverish conditions. It is not habit forming and has been given as a substitute for narcotic drugs.

HIGH BLOOD PRESSURE: When high blood pressure is due to mental nervous conditions, this herb will help to remedy the condition by removing the nervous condition.

NEURALGIA: This pain, in the area of nerves, is often relieved by the use of this herb.

HEADACHES: When headaches are due to nervous conditions, the use of this herb will usually relieve the headache.

ASTHMA: In the condition known as spasmodic asthma, caused by emotional disturbances, this herb will usually give relief.

DOSAGES: One herbal recommends ten to twenty drops of the fluid extract as a dosage. A dose of the dry powder would be not more than three grains, twice daily.

PILEWORT

**Also known as Small Celandine,
Lesser Celandine.**

Botanical name: Ranunculus Ficaria

Effects and reported uses: The principal effect of this herb is in connection with treatment of hemorrhoids or piles.

It is an astringent, drawing the tissues together and halting discharges of body fluids. For external use, the entire herb is softened by soaking it in boiling lard for twenty-four hours at a temperature of one hundred degrees Fahrenheit. The resulting ointment gives reportedly beneficial results. For internal use, a pint of boiling water is poured over an ounce of the powdered herb. One-half cup may be taken twice daily.

PINK ROOT

Other names are American Worm Root, Worm Grass, Spigelia, Maryland Pinkroot, Carolina Pinkroot, India Pink, Demerara Pinkroot.

Botanical name: Spigelia Marilandica, or Spigelia. In France, it is called Spigelie du Maryland and in Germany it is referred to as Spigelie.

Habitat: It is found in the United States in the rich woods of the eastern states to Kentucky, and south to Florida and Texas. Most of the root is now being obtained from Mississippi.

Growth needs: Rich soil, ample water and temperate climate. Plenty of sunshine is needed but growth in a partially shaded area would be best.

Description: This herb has two portions, the underground and the aerial parts. Being a perennial plant, it grows

constantly throughout the year. The underground portion
consists of slender branched roots with numerous long
slender fibrous roots. The aerial stems attain a height of
from twelve to twenty-four inches. The leaves are oval
shaped and they grow on the stem opposite to each other.
Flowers are tubular-funnel-shaped and appear at the end of
the stem from May to July. The flower is scarlet red on the
outside and yellow within.

Physiological effect: This herb has a volatile quality;
that is, it evaporates easily at ordinary temperatures, as it
contains volatile oils. Having a nitrogenous organic base
and being a volatile alkaloid, there is a powerful toxic effect
on the animal structure. Apparently the substance of this
plant, containing a toxic oil, attacks the intestinal worms
and either destroys or weakens them, thus expelling or
tending to expel them. It is reported advisable to combine
this herb with an effective laxative such as Senna.

Conditions for which reportedly used: For intestinal
worms.

Precautions. When seeking to expel worms from the
intestines, it is well to avoid any heavy eating and to avoid
breakfast prior to partaking of the herb. Lemon juice may
be taken freely before and after use of the herb.

Preparation. The whole plant is used or the root itself
may be used. An infusion is made by pouring hot water over
the powdered root or plant. In the case of children, the
mixture should be about one ounce of the powder to one
pint of the hot water. The mixture may be sweetened and

given to the child in tablespoonful doses morning and evening. For an adult, the dose may be up to a small cupful of the mixture instead of a tablespoonful. This dose may be repeated both morning and night for three or four days.

PITCHER PLANT

Also known as Fly Trap, Water Cup, Saddleplant.

Botanical name: Sarracenia purpurea.

Effects and reported uses: The powdered root of this plant has been found to serve as an effective preventive of smallpox and it is also used to help cure smallpox when it occurs. It has also been found to be useful in various derangements of the stomach, liver and kidneys and is valuable for constipation and dyspepsia, the medical term for incomplete digestion. It is also a laxative and a diuretic, increasing kidney activity and increasing the flow of urine. A pint of boiling water is poured over an ounce of the powdered root and allowed to steep for several minutes. Dosage is from one tablespoonful to one-half cup, taken twice daily.

PLANTAIN

Also known as Ripple Grass, Waybread.

Botanical name: Plantago major.

Effects and reported uses: The leaves of this herb have a cooling effect upon the body and also stop bleeding from minor wounds. The fresh leaves may be rubbed directly on parts of the body stung by insects or on the skin rash produced by the stinging nettle, a plant with tiny or minute stinging hairs. The irritation results from an irritating watery juice discharged by the hairs when broken. Internally, the herb is reported beneficial for cases of diarrhea and for piles. The internal solution is prepared by pouring a pint of boiling water over an ounce of the dried powdered leaves. An average dose is one-half cup taken twice daily.

QUEEN'S DELIGHT

This is also known as Queen's Root, Yaw Root and Silver Leaf.

Botanical name: Stillingia sylvatica Linne, also as Euphorbiacae. The French and German name is Stillingie.

Habitat: It is found in the southeastern United States, from Virginia to Florida.

Growth needs: This is a plant that is constantly growing (perennial) and therefore needs a warm climate as frost will destroy the plant. A fairly ample supply of water is needed as well as considerable sunshine and fertile soil.

Description: This is a monoecious herb, having stamens and pistils in separate blossoms on the same plant. The underground root has several branches of slender shape. A smooth erect stem rises from the root, which is from three-quarters to two inches thick and several inches in length. The leaves are pointed (lanceolate) and have irregular edges like saw teeth (serrated) with flowers that are yellow with terminal spikes. The fruit is a rough, greenish-brown, three-celled capsule, each cell containing a single seed. The part used in herbology is the dried root, which has an outer covering of cork that surrounds a large area of tubular long conveyors called phloem. In the center of the root, there is an area of very narrow tubular rays called medullary rays only one to two cells wide. These are also referred to as tracheids, or elongated woody cells of a slightly woody nature. The outer covering of cork has cells of a definitely woody nature.

Conditions for which reportedly used: Standard herbals recommend this herb for purifying blood conditions such as syphilis and scrofula. Scrofula is a tendency toward inflammation of the skin, mucous membrane and joints. This term (scrofula) is also used to indicate glandular tumors, usually in the neck, that degenerate into ulcers. Queen's Delight is used to restore a normal condition in the blood system and tends to help remove any infectious disease.

IN COMBINATION: This herb is often used with other herbs for various results. It is combined with the herb known as Sundew as a cough remedy or for laryngitis; with bittersweet for eczema and as a relaxant; with milkweed and Indian Tobacco for bronchitis.

PREPARATION. One-eighth of an ounce of the powdered root is sufficient for the preparation of one dose, which

would be sufficient for an entire day. It may be taken with
some fruit juice or may be placed in a capsule and swallowed without the taste or odor affecting the senses.

OTHER USES. This herb has also been recommended
as a laxative and as a diuretic, stimulating action of the kidneys, and stimulating the secretion of urine.

QUINCE

**Also known as Cydonium,
Quince Seed, Semen Cydoniae,
Cydonia vulgaris.**

Foreign names: German, Quittensamen; French, Se-
mences de Coing.

Botanical names: Cydonia oblonga, Pyrus Cydonia;
Rose family (Rosaceae)

Habitat: Asia. Also cultivated in the United States and
Europe.

Growth needs: Fairly good soil, ample water and sun.

Description: A shrub or small tree with slender branches.
Leaves are oval or oblong with hairy under-surfaces. Flowers are white or light pink. The fruits are globular and somewhat hairy before maturity.

Part used: Seeds. The fruits are gathered in autumn when mature, crushed, and the seeds removed and dried.

Effects: Contracts tissues and skin.

Recorded uses: Used as a soothing lotion in eye diseases, such as conjunctivitis. It is also of value in loose bowels of diarrhea and dysentery. The macerated seeds, when mixed with water, are claimed to be valuable for healing abrasions of the skin and fissures or cracks in mucous membrane.

Recorded cosmetic uses: A mixture of the seeds (two parts seeds to one hundred parts of water) results in a lotion that is excellent for the skin. When allowed to remain on the skin overnight, the skin will tend to contract and, temporarily at least, lessen wrinkles. Another value for this lotion is on the hair, as a hair dressing to hold stray hairs in place.

Recorded food value: The quince, when ripe, is a nutritious edible fruit.

RED ROOT

Also known as Jersey Tea Root.

Botanical name: Ceanothus Americanus.

Effects and reported uses: The root of this herb has an astringent effect, drawing the tissues together and checking secretions issuing from the mucous membrane. It is also an expectorant, helping to remove secretions from the mucous membrane of the broncho-pulmonary passages. It is also anti-spasmodic, in tending to stop spasms of the mucous membranes as in cases of asthma and other pulmonary complaints. A pint of boiling water over an ounce of the powdered root will produce an extract that can be used for internal treatments of the foregoing ailments. Also, the solution makes an excellent mouthwash for any mouth sores. For internal use, a small amount will suffice to obtain the desired results. Usually a teaspoonful taken three times daily will be sufficient.

RED SAGE

Also known as Garden Sage.

Botanical name: Salvia officinalis.

Effects and reported uses: The leaves of this plant are used to produce an aromatic fragrance that has many healthful values. A solution that is taken internally and is also used as a gargle has an astringent effect, drawing tissues together and halting the discharge of body secretions. The solution is prepared by pouring one-half pint of hot malt vinegar upon one ounce of the leaves, either whole but preferably in powdered form. One-half pint of cold water is then added to the solution. The internal dose is one-half cup at a time, taken twice daily. Both the gargle and the internal drink relieves laryngitis, sore throat, infected tonsils and ulcers of the mouth and throat. Sage is also used for culinary taste purposes.

RHATANY, PERUVIAN

Also known as Rhatanhia.

Botanical name: Krameria triandra.

Effects and reported uses: This herb is both an astringent and a tonic. It draws tissue together and reduces discharges from tissues. It is also a tonic, restoring strength and tone to the muscles. It is used in hemorrhages to stop bleeding and is useful in other discharges of mucus from the mucous membranes. It has been found beneficial in menstrual disorders where discharge of fluids occurs, and it has also been found valuable in cases of diarrhea to restore normal functioning of the bowels. It is also of value in cases of incontinence of urine, a condition of inability to retain urine through loss of sphincter or muscle control. This herb is also useful in cases of spongy or bleeding gums, associated with the condition known as pyorrhea. One-half teaspoon of the powdered root is a sufficient dose for internal use. A small amount of the powder may be applied directly to the gums for treatment of the gums.

RHUBARB

Also known as Rheum, Rhubarb Root, Turkey or Chinese Rhubarb, Rhizoma Rhei.

Botanical name: Rheum officinale, Rheum palmatum of the Family Polygonaceae.

Habitat: The original species, in China and Tibet, has been in use for medicinal purposes from 2700 B.C. The rhubarb cultivated in the United States is devoid of cathartic power and the domestic leaf-stalks are used as a fruit. It is commonly grown in many areas of the world as a popular farm product. Medicinal rhubarb comes largely from Turkey, India and England.

Growth needs: Ample water supply, good soil and fair amount of sunshine. Soil should be treated with well-rotted manure.

Description: This herb resembles the ordinary garden variety of rhubarb, but attains a larger size. The above-ground portion of the plant has a number of long stalks that are leaf-like in appearance, rising from the rhizome or portion of stem of the plant just below the ground. Greenish white flowers appear in the spring. The root is fleshy and of a spreading character.

Parts used: The dried rhizomes and roots, without the bark-like covering.

Effects: Cathartic and astringent.

Recorded uses: It has been long used for cleansing the alimentary canal and has the characteristic effect of following the cleansing action with an astringent or contracting action, tending to diminish discharge. The average recommended dose of the powdered roots is one gram or fifteen grains for the purgative effect and about one-third of this amount or five grains if it is desired only to obtain the astringent or contracting effect to diminish diarrhea. The small dose of perhaps three-grain size has been used in caring for small infants suffering from looseness of the bowels. Another use for rhubarb is the action of acting as a tonic on the stomach, improving the digestive organs and creating an appetite. Rhubarb is recognized as the most mild of laxatives and is especially recommended in convalescence from exhausting diseases. The entire intestinal canal is cleansed including the duodenum or small intestine. The gentle action of this herb makes it especially desirable in cases of persons bothered with hemorrhoids. The astringent effect may be avoided by taking a teaspoonful of olive oil at night.

ROSEMARY

Also known as Romero.

Botanical name: Rosmarinus officinalis.

Effects and reported uses: This herb is a tonic, strengthening and toning the muscles. It is also an astringent, drawing tissues together and causing a cessation of fluid discharges. In addition, it is a diaphoretic, increasing perspiration. It has excellent effects on the stomach, increasing action in the stomach. It acts as a nervine, lessening irritability of the nerves, and serves as a nerve sedative. In this regard, it has been effective in relieving headaches. It has also been recommended for use in preventing premature baldness by combining a solution of this herb with Borax. The oil of the herb is used for treatments, with two to three drops of the oil sufficient for a dose. For the hair treatment, pour a pint of boiling water over an ounce of the dried herb or powder and mix the solution with Borax in the proportion of one tablespoonful of Borax to a cup of the solution.

SARSAPARILLA

Also known as (1) Mexican, Vera Cruz, Tampico or Gray Sarsaparilla; (2) Honduras or Brown Sarsaparilla; (3) Ecuadorian Sarsaparilla. Other names are Central American, Jamaica, Costa Rica, Lima or Red Sarsaparilla or Quay-quill Sarsaparilla, Red Sarsaparilla, Bindweed, Small Spikenard, Spignet, China Root.

Botanical names: Smilax aristolochioefolia; Smilax medica; Smilax Regalii; Smilax officinalis; Aralia Nudicaulis, Smilax Ornata, Smilax China.

Habitat: Tropical areas of Central and South America; also in China and Japan.

Growth needs: Hot and humid climate with good soil and good water supply.

Description: Climbing evergreen shrubs with prickly stems. The leaves are round to oblong and are usually armed with spines on the lower side. The fruit is a small, globular berry.

Part used: The dried root.

Effects: This herb has been widely reported as an alterative, tending to restore an abnormal system to normalcy.

Recorded uses: This herb has a long record of use for the relief of pain in the head or pain in various joints of the body. It is also held in high repute as a purifier of the blood and has had considerable use in coping with syphilis infections. It is also regarded as an aphrodisiac and has been used successfully in scrofula (tuberculous disease of lymphatic glands and of bone, usually with abscesses), chronic rheumatism and diseases of the skin. It is reported to be best used in the form of a decoction, with one ounce of the root boiled in one pint of water for one-half hour. Frequent doses of approximately one wine glassful should be taken. It is excellent, according to many sources, for gout and for ringworm, the parasitic skin disease which shows as circular patches. It has been recommended as an excellent antidote to remove the effects of any strong poison; however, before taking, the stomach should first be cleansed. It is said to be excellent for colds, running nose and fever and promotes profuse perspiration when taken hot. It is also a good eyewash. It is also powerful enough to expel gas from the stomach and bowels. The powdered herb may be mixed with food for internal use.

SASSAFRAS

**This is the dried bark of the
root of Sassafras variifolium of
the botanical order Lauraceae.
It is also known as Ague Tree,
saxifrax, cinnamon wood, saloip.**

Botanical name: Sassafras officinale.

Habitat: Found in the rich woods of the United States,
mainly in Virginia, Kentucky, Tennessee and Kansas. No
doubt, the tree will grow in any area of rich soil with ample
water and sunlight.

Description: Sassafras is the dried bark of the root of
an indigenous tree, collected in early spring or autumn, at
which time the outer bark is removed. The height of the
tree varies from ten feet to one hundred feet in height. The
leaves are ovate (egg-shaped) and the flowers are greenish-
yellow. The blue fruit is round and borne on the end of a
thick reddish stalk.

Part used: The dried bark of the root. Another process
involves taking the tree stump, reducing it to small chips
and therefrom distilling oil from the stump.

Effects: Effective as a stimulant; destroys certain pro-
tozoa; has an agreeable spicy odor; increases perspiration;
relieves toothache; helps clear skin affections; stimulates
activity of the kidneys.

Recorded uses: The oil of the sassafras tree has many uses, both internally and when applied externally. When taken internally, it is reported to purify the blood and cleanse the entire system. An ounce of the crushed bark steeped in a pint of boiling water, taken in doses of a wine glassful and repeated frequently is the customary dose. If the oil itself is used, a dosage of one to five drops in water that has been boiled is usually satisfactory. Various source books indicate this herb is excellent for various skin conditions as well as for varicose vein ulcers. It is recommended for inflamed eyes, rheumatism, gout, and syphilitic infections. It is reported as useful as a tonic for the stomach and the bowels. Taken warm, it is reported to relieve spasms. Other uses include use as a flavoring agent and as a repellent for ants. It is also used as an antiseptic spray for the nose and throat.

SAW PALMETTO

Botanical names: Seronoa serrulata and Sabal serrulata.

Effects and reported uses: The berries of this plant, fresh or dried, have been recommended in diseases that enfeeble the body and cause loss of strength and size. This plant has a marked effect upon glandular tissues, resulting in increase in weight and increasing strength and tone of muscles. It is therefore considered to be a nutritive tonic and has been successfully used in tuberculosis cases. It is also recommended for improving and increasing the func-

tion and size of the mammary glands. For the men, this herb
is also recommended for improving the functions of the
glandular bodies in the scrotum of the male, the testes.
If taken fresh, from three to five berries is sufficient for a
dose, taken three times daily. If dried berries or the powder
of dried berries is used, a solution may be prepared by taking an ounce of the dried berries or powder and pouring one-
half pint of boiling water over the herb. After steeping for
several minutes, an average dose should be one teaspoonful
three times daily.

SCOPOLIS

Botanical name: Scopola Carniolica and also Scopolia
Atropoides.

Effects and reported uses: This herb has a sedative effect
upon nerves and muscles of the body. When taken, examina-
tion of the pupils of the eye will show dilatation or wide
opening of the pupils. It has been found valuable for relief
of pain and relieves coughs. It also suppresses glandular
secretions. Only a small amount is necessary for action. The
powdered root may be taken in dried form in a dose of from
one to five grains. Usually an amount equivalent to about
one-quarter of an ordinary seven-grain tablet is sufficient
for good effect. A liquid solution may be prepared by pouring one-half pint of boiling water over an ounce of the powder and allowing the solution to steep for about ten minutes.
The dose of the liquid solution should be from one to five
drops in a small quantity of water.

SCULLCAP

**Also known as Skullcap, Mad-
weed.**

Botanical name: Scutellaria lateriflora.

Effects and reported uses: The powdered herb has been recommended for special nervous conditions and is also recommended as a nerve tonic for almost all disorders of the nervous system. It has been reportedly successful in hysteria, convulsions, St. Vitus' Dance and similar ailments, including hydrophobia or rabies. It has a slightly astringent effect, tending to reduce discharge of body fluid and drawing tissues together. A pint of boiling water is poured over an ounce of the powder to make the solution. The dosage is one tablespoonful at a time taken five or six times a day or more often until the condition improves. The dosage may then be reduced to three times daily to maintain improvement.

SENNA

**Other names are Senna Leaves,
Alexandrian Senna, East Indian
Senna, Tinnevelly Senna, Indian
Senna and American Senna.**

Botanical names: Cassia angustifolia Vahl and Cassia acutifolia Delilea. The French name for this herb is Sene de Tinnevelly and in the German language Indische Senna.

Habitat: The original habitat is Africa, in the middle and upper Nile areas. It is also found in the Mediterranean areas and in India. American Senna has been grown in Massachusetts to Ohio and in Tennessee and North Carolina.

Growth needs: It is known to grow in swampy places, therefore indicating the need for a location with plenty of water as well as sunshine. It is known to grow in northern climates, as well as in warm climates. Good rich soil would be considered necessary.

Description: The senna leaves grow on a low shrub with branched whitish stems. The leaves are rather small, varying from one-half to one and one-half inches long and from one-quarter to one-half inch broad. The leaves are greyish green and shaped like the head of a lance, with a point both at the tip of the leaf and at the base. Pods form on the bush, with six or seven seeds. One of the varieties has eight seeds.

Physiological effect: This herb has an irritating effect upon the muscles of the colon, producing increased peristalsis or forwarding movement.

Conditions for which reportedly used:

AS A LAXATIVE OR CLEANSER OF THE BOWELS: It is more purgative than a laxative and more mild than any drastic means of emptying the bowels. It is sometimes combined with aromatics and stimulants in order to modify the strong effect.

FORMULA FOR INFUSION: Two ounces of senna leaves in one pint of boiling water. Allow to stand for one hour. Strain through muslin and drink in doses of about a wine glassful every few hours until there is a thorough internal cleaning action. Some ginger may be added with the senna leaves. About one-eighth of an ounce would be sufficient.

AS A TEA: The senna leaves or powder may be used as a tea drink, preparing in the same manner as above. Rhubarb may be used as an additional component with the senna. Another ingredient often used with senna is the bark of the cascara buck-thorn, a small tree of the northwest United States and Canada, known as cascara sagrada. Dr. Nicolas Burney, famous naturopathic physician, has combined cascara bark, jalap root, anise seed and licorice root with the senna to produce a mild and effective laxative.

SIMARUBA

Also known as Mountain Damson.

Botanical name: Simaruba officinalis.

Effects and reported uses: This herb is helpful for cases of loss of appetite, especially where a patient is recovering during a period of convalescence from illness. It is of special value for aiding the digestive processes. One-half ounce of the powdered bark of the root is used to one pint of boiling water. The dose is from one to two tablespoons every three hours, until improvement is noted. This drink is a tonic that will strengthen the muscles and tone the tissues.

SLIPPERY ELM

Other names for this herb are
Red Elm and Moose Elm.

Botanical name: Ulmus Fulva. In French it is called Ecorce d'Orme and in the German language, Ulmenrinde.

Habitat: It is found generally in the area of Quebec in the east to North Dakota in the west and thence southward to Florida and Texas. Most of the supply comes from the state of Michigan.

Growth needs: The growth of this substance requires a substantial amount of rainfall, alternating shade and sunshine conditions and fairly rich soil.

Description: The Slippery Elm trees attain a height of fifty to sixty feet with a trunk diameter of one to two and one-half feet. Branches are stout and reach upwards and have a flat-topped crown. The bark of the tree is thick, tough, dark brown and longitudinally fissured. The part used in herbology is the dried inner bark, which is fragrant and mucilaginous. Flowers usually appear in April, before the leaves. The leaves are dark green and sharply pointed. The surface of the leaf has small elevations or rough spots. The edges of the leaves have points like a saw and the point edges themselves also have points in them, known as doubly serrated leaves.

Physiological effect: This herb contains mucilage cells as well as starch, tannin and calcium oxalate. This substance penetrates exposed and irritated surfaces and covers the surface and thus aids in the healing processes. It tends to soften and relax inflamed tissue, having what is known as an emollient effect.

Reported uses:

INFLAMED CONDITIONS OF MUCOUS MEMBRANES OF STOMACH, BOWELS AND KIDNEYS: Steep two or more ounces of slippery elm bark in a quart of boiling water for an hour or longer. After straining, it may be taken freely. It may also be mixed with honey or simple syrup for sweeter taste. A teaspoon every half hour will soothe the membranes.

ENEMAS: When taken as an enema, it is soothing to the lower bowels when inflammation is present.

VAGINAL DOUCHES: This herb is recommended for inflammation of the vagina. For a douche or for an enema, it is necessary to use a lighter mixture, using only one ounce of the cut bark instead of two ounces. It should be steeped in a quart of boiling water for an hour and then strained. It is then ready for use.

AS A FOOD: Some herb authorities recommend this herb as a food. The bark is ground into a powder and prepared like a cereal with either water or milk. It has been recommended for general weakness and other conditions such as bleeding of the lungs, bronchitis, or tuberculosis. When taken as a food for infants, a teaspoonful of the powder, mixed with the same amount of powdered sugar and added to one pint of boiling water, will make a nutritious and healthful formula for the baby. Cinnamon or nutmeg may be added for taste.

AS A POULTICE: The coarse powder, mixed with water, makes a poultice that has had wonderful results for many skin ailments, including burns, boils, ulcers and wounds.

SNAKE ROOT

Also known as Virginia Snakeroot, Red River Snakeroot, Texas Snakeroot.

Botanical names: Aristolochia Serpentaria, Aristolochia reticulata.

Effects and reported uses: This is considered a fever remedy, especially in cases of typhoid fever. It has the effect of increasing perspiration and it is a stimulant, promoting activity of the various glands of the body. It is also a pain reliever and an anti-spasmodic, tending to reduce or halt spasms. It is a tonic, strengthening muscles and the tissues. It has been recommended for bilious conditions marked by headache, constipation, loss of appetite and vomiting of bile.

To make a solution of the herb, take a pint of boiling water and pour it over one-half ounce of the powdered root. One to two tablespoonfuls may be taken at a time two or three times daily.

SOAP TREE

Also known as Soap Bark, Panama Bark, Quillaia.

Botanical name: Quillaja Saponaria.

Effects and reported uses: This is considered to be a remedy for relief of coughs in chronic bronchitis and other lung complaints. A pint of boiling water is poured over one-half ounce of the powdered bark for a solution of this remedy. It is taken a tablespoonful at a time as needed to relieve the symptoms. The same solution may be used as an external cleanser for ulcers or other eruptions of the skin. It also has the effect of a diuretic, promoting action of the kidneys and the flow of urine.

TANSY

Also known as Common Tansy, Hindheel, Arbor Vitae, Yellow Cedar.

Botanical name: Tanacetum Vulgare of the Family Compositae.

Habitat: Originally known as a native of Europe, it is now found in the United States.

Growth needs: Grows fast from seed under almost any conditions.

Description: Approximately three feet tall, this herb bears yellow flowers in the late summer. The leaflets are rich green in color and arranged in a fernlike pattern. The stems are slightly hairy. The leaves are from six to eight inches in length and about four inches wide, with about twelve segments on each side.

Parts used: The dried leaves and the flowering tops.

Effects: Promotes menstrual flow; also an irritant and a narcotic.

Recorded uses: This herb is prepared by steeping an ounce of the herb with one pint of boiling water. Two table-spoonfuls at a time, repeated frequently, will give quick results. When menstruation has been delayed for causes other than pregnancy, this herb has been used for many years to bring about menstruation. Pregnant women should not use it as it may cause a miscarriage or an abortion. It has also been widely used to destroy abdominal worms, in which case food should be kept to a minimum and doses taken morning and night. It has also been used for relief in cases of slow and painful discharge of urine. When taken cold, it is re-garded as a stimulating tonic, for men or for women, and is an aid to digestion. Physicians have recommended it for strengthening weak veins and kidneys. The oil of tansy is powerful and the dosage is from one to three drops.

WARNING: Any overdoses of either the oil or boiled preparations of the herb may have possible fatal results. Another herbal authority states that Tansy has never been known to fail to cure palpitation of the heart in a few days. Another authority acclaims Tansy as a good medicine for pains in the back and in the loins (between the pelvis and chest area). Another old herbal refers to the common usage of applying the herb externally to the abdominal area of women in the vicinity of the navel to prevent miscarriages. Tansy is also said to heal ulcers in the mouth or other parts of the body and is said to cleanse the skin of pimples, freckles or effects of sunburns, taking away the heat and inflammation.

TURPENTINE

Also known as Gum Thus, Crede Turpentine, Gum Turpentine, Lump Turpentine.

Foreign names: German, Terpentin; French, Terebenthine commune.

Botanical names: Pinus palustris; Pinus Maritima of the family of Pinaceae.

Habitat: In southern United States from Virginia to Florida, and in Texas.

Growth needs: Rich soil, ample water and sun.

Description: A large evergreen tree with thin scaly cork and hard resinous wood, growing mainly within one hundred miles of the coast. The leaves are in clusters of three and range from five to ten inches in length. The cone scales are long and flattened, with short, sharp and recurved spines.

Part used: Product formed in the wood of the trees, flowing from cuts into bark.

Effects: Tends to develop new tissue; stimulates; antiseptic.

Recorded uses: Oil of turpentine has been successfully used upon the urinary apparatus, and has been found valuable in chronic diseased conditions of the kidneys and bladder, including gonorrhea. It is also reported as favorable for treatment of diseases of the mucous membranes of the respiratory organs. The oil is also used often in liniments for rheumatism and chest complaints, as well as for strains and sprains. It is recognized as having the ability to stop bleeding, apparently by compression of the blood vessels. It has also been used in combination with castor oil to destroy tapeworms in the intestines, the castor oil passing the substance rapidly through the intestines. The pure vapor of oil of turpentine is an irritant and provokes coughing, causing the expulsion of morbid products in cases of bronchitis and pneumonia.

CAUTIONARY NOTE: The internal use of oil of turpentine is dangerous and any excess dosage may cause severe illness or death. There are various preparations of turpentine and the exact manner of preparation is the work of a chemist or pharmacist.

Terebene: Concentrated sulphuric acid acts on oil of turpentine to produce the liquid known as terebene. It has been reported as a remedy for coughs and in solution with cocaine as a spray for hay-fever. It is also valued as an inhalant for chronic bronchitis and similar ailments.

WHITE BRYONY

Also known as Bryonia, English Mandrake, Wild Vine, Mandragora, Bryony Root, Bryony, Bryonin, European White Bryony, Wild Bryony.

Botanical name: Bryonia alba and Bryonia dioica. Family: Cucurbitacae.

Habitat: Europe.

Growth needs: Temperate climate. Fairly good soil. Ample water and sun.

Description: Perennial climbing vine. Leaves are five-lobed with small greenish-white to yellowish flowers. The variety known as Alba have black fruit and the dioica variety have red fruit berries. Roots are spindle-shaped and from one to two feet in length. The diameter of the root is from one to three inches. The root is white in color externally and internally.

Part used: Root.

Effects: Cathartic (cleansing) action. Irritating.

Recorded uses: Has been used to increase flow of urine (diuretic). The average dose of this herb is fifteen grains. It may be prepared as a tincture by taking an ounce of the powdered herb and diluting it with a pint of pure grain alcohol. A dose of the tincture would be one teaspoonful morning and night. Other recorded uses of this herb are:

PLEURISY: Tends to clear lungs and remove pain.

DROPSY: Tends to remove excess fluids from glands.

BRONCHITIS: Tends to clear bronchial tubes.

TONSILITIS: Tends to reduce swelling of glands.

HEART DISEASE: Tends to normalize heart conditions brought about by inflammation due to rheumatism or gout.

COUGHS: Has been found valuable for removing irritations in bronchial tubes and lungs causing coughs.

INFLUENZA: Aid in cases of influenza by clearing bronchial tubes and lungs.

PNEUMONIA: Cleanses lungs and therefore has been found valuable in pneumonia cases.

WITCH-HAZEL

Also known as Hamamelis, Winter-bloom, Striped Elder, Spotted Elder, Hazel-nut, Snapping Hazel, Pistachio, Tobacco Wood, Witch-hazel Leaves.

Botanical name: Hamamelis virginiana of the family Hamamelidaceae.

Habitat: Found in damp woodlands of North America from Nova Scotia to Florida and westward to Minnesota and Texas.

Growth needs: Ample water, rich soil and fair amount of sunshine.

Description: A rather tall shrub or small tree that may reach a height of ten or twelve feet. The trunk is crooked and may be as thick as a man's arm. Flowers are yellow-petaled. The fruit is a woody two-seeded capsule. The leaves are round and grow alternately on the stems.

Parts used: The dried leaf. The bark and twigs are also used. Small branches have been used as divining rods to locate water.

Effects: Tends to stop bleeding; also has a stimulating effect and is a sedative.

Recorded uses: Witch-hazel has been taken internally and applied externally for hemorrhoids, especially of the bleeding variety. It has been used for varicose veins, ulcers, bleeding from the nose, stomach, lungs, rectum and kidneys. It has been a long-time remedy for sprains and bruises as well as for cleansing of foul ulcerated parts of the body. It has been found to be valuable for treatment of gonorrhea as well as for treatment of leucorrhea, a condition of discharge of a greenish-white mucus from the female genital organs. It is also valuable in sore throat treatments, as witch-hazel draws tissues together to halt or diminish discharge from the tissues. It has been recommended for use in stopping excessive menstruation. It is useful in cases of diarrhea, the witch-hazel being taken either internally as an enema or entering the system by a dose of thirty grains of the powdered dried leaves repeated every four hours or preparing a distilled extract of the dried twigs or leaves. Various manufacturers sell so-called distilled extracts that are in some cases really waters distilled from the bark. Some witch-hazel ointments are also on the market. Many of the solutions contain alcohol to preserve the valuable properties of witch-hazel.

SPICE AND HERB COOKERY

Many people enjoy the health benefits of herbs without realizing it. Throughout their lives they have become accustomed to the use of herbs and spices to give foods and beverages a flavor and zest otherwise absent. According to the dictionary, a spice is merely an herb with an aromatic fragrance or a pungent taste, such as cinnamon, cloves, pepper, nutmeg, allspice and mace. The list that follows, therefore, is a list of aromatic herbs or spices, if you please, in common or uncommon use in the flavoring of foods and beverages with a table of uses.

SPICE OR HERB	USES
ALFALFA	As a tea. Leaves are rich with vitamins and minerals.
ALLSPICE	This has long been used for flavoring cakes, frostings, puddings, soups, jellies, sauces, pickles, etc.
ANISE	The seeds are used in flavoring cookies, pastries, soup, beets, salads and beverages.
ASAFETIDA	General flavoring, meats, fish and soups.
BASIL	May be used fresh or dried with tomatoes, poultry, meat, game, fish, eggs, soups and sauces.
BAY LEAVES	Used with soups, stews, beef roasts, gravies, sauces, pickles, etc.
BEE BALM	This is also known as Oswego Tea. It is an Indian tea origi-

SPICE OR HERB	USES
	nally used in northern New England.
BLUE MOUNTAIN	This is a delicious and harmless substitute for China teas.
CARAWAY	May be used to flavor roast goose, duck and pork. It is also popular in the bakery line, covering black bread, salt rolls and bread sticks.
CARDAMON SEEDS	This seed is used for flavoring cookies, cakes, candies, curry powders and beverages. In some areas, the seeds are placed in coffee for better flavor.
CATNIP	As an old-fashioned tea it is served with lemon and is an old-time favorite.
CELERY SEEDS	Used for flavoring catsup, pickles, soups, French dressings, salads, sauces, gravies, cabbage and beet dishes.
CHAMOMILE FLOWERS	As a smooth tea it is considered very soothing.
CHERVIL	Appearance is similar to parsley but it is similar to tarragon in flavor. It may be used fresh

SPICE OR HERB	USES
	or dried in salads, soups and with fish and eggs.
CHICORY, ROASTED	This is used to add flavor to coffee and is sometimes used alone as a coffee substitute.
CHIVES	This has a mild onion flavor. It is commonly used when fresh but it is also available as a frozen item. It is frequently used in salads or as a sauce mixed with butter, lemon juice or sour cream. It is also sprinkled over vegetables.
CINNAMON	Used on appetizers such as cranberry sauce, picked or spiced fruits, pickles and catsup. The whole pieces of bark are used with pickles and with chutney. It is also sprinkled as a powder over ham, lamb, pork chops, lamb or beef stews and is used as part of goose stuffing. It is also sprinkled over fruits and desserts and beverages such as all milk drinks, custard, fruit or rice puddings and pumpkin, apple, peach, cream or custard pies. It is popular used as pieces of

SPICE OR HERB	USES
	the bark with heated wine and in hot tea, coffee, hot chocolate drinks and in spiced and pickled fruits.
CLOVER FLOWERS	This is considered as producing a healthful tea, especially when alfalfa and peppermint leaves are added.
CLOVES	Excellent for sprinkling over baked fish, scrambled or creamed eggs, beets, sweet potatoes, tomatoes, spaghetti, chili, wine and all spice cakes, cookies and puddings. Whole cloves are used in the marinade or soaking solution for beef, pork, lamb or veal, as well as in stock for boiling meat loaf or poultry.
CORIANDER SEEDS	Used in flavoring bakery pastries, confections, sausage, pickles, beverages, etc.
CUMIN SEEDS	These seeds are used in flavoring pastries, soups, salads, meats, cheese, sauerkraut and spicy dishes and are also used generally for sprinkling over baked products.

SPICE OR HERB	USES
DILL HERB	The herb plant itself is used for pickling and is also popular for preparation of beef sauce, boiled fish, bean soup, etc. The young leaves are used for seasoning salads and are sometimes stirred into mayonnaise.
DILL SEEDS	These seeds are used in flavoring vinegar, pickles, sauces, gravies, soups, fish, etc.
FENNEL SEEDS	These seeds are used in flavoring black bread, sauerkraut, soups, fish and sauces.
GARDEN BURNET	These fresh cucumber-like scented leaves are used in soups, salads and cooling drinks.
GARDEN MARJORAM	This has a sweet, spicy flavor and may be used fresh or dried, with lamb, cheese dishes, fish, eggs and soups. It should not be cooked for more than a few minutes.
GARLIC	This adds a delicious mild flavor to salads when rubbed on the salad bowl. It is excellent with pork or beef. It may be

SPICE OR HERB	USES
	rubbed on the meat or small pieces may be inserted.
GINGER	An excellent flavoring. It may be sprinkled on broiled or baked fish, pot roast, steak, lamb, candied sweet potatoes, glazed carrots or onions, winter squash. It is also fine for sprinkling on sauces for pork, veal and fish and is highly relished for addition to marinades for beef, lamb, chicken and turkey. It is also fine for sprinkling on canned fruit, steamed puddings, and bread or rice puddings. It is an important ingredient in gingerbread, gingersnaps and ginger cookies.
HYSSOP	The fresh tips are used in salads to impart a bitterish taste.
MACE	Used in appetizers and garnishes such as pickles, fruit preserves and jellies. It is sprinkled on trout and scalloped fish as well as rabbit, lamb chops and sausage. It is especially tasteful for use on such vegetables as buttered carrots,

SPICE OR HERB	USES
	cauliflower, squash, Swiss chard and spinach. It is also tasty on creamed or mashed potatoes and is usually an important ingredient in sauces used for fish, veal and chicken. It is sprinkled on cooked apples, cherries, prunes and apricots and tastes good on pancakes and chocolate pudding. It is often sprinkled on cottage or custard puddings. Mace is more delicate in flavor than nutmeg. It is the outer covering of the nutmeg kernel and is often used like nutmeg.
MUSTARD SEEDS	The black seed is stronger than the white. They are both used in sauces, pickles and curry powders. Ground mustard seed is especially good with sage when rubbed on pork roast.
NUTMEG	This is used as a garnish for milk, chocolate and spiced drinks. It is excellent for baked croquettes and is popular for use with Swedish meat balls, meat loaf and meat pie. It is also widely used for sprinkling

SPICE OR HERB	USES

on chicken and is excellent for the vegetables for which mace has been indicated to be well suited. Nutmeg is popular in sauces prepared for chicken, seafood and veal. It is also sprinkled on ice cream, cakes, cookies and puddings.

OREGANO

This spice is used to flavor soups, stews, omelettes and pizza. It is also used with creamed vegetables and salads.

PAPRIKA

Paprika is rich in Vitamin C and gives a sweet flavor to many dishes including ground beef and all cheese mixtures. It is frequently used in dipping mixtures for fried chicken and in mixtures for pork chops and veal cutlets. It is a pleasant addition to the baked potato and is frequently used for sprinkling on sour cream, salad dressings and cream sauce. It is often used routinely for sprinkling on hors d'oeuvres and on the bread fried in butter and served with hors d'oeuvres, known as canapes.

SPICE OR HERB	USES
PEPPERCORNS	A berry or two gives zest to beef, pot roast, corned beef and gravies. It is also used in pickling processes.
POPPY SEEDS	Used on cookies, cakes, bread, rolls, etc.
ROSEMARY	This is ideal for seasoning creamed soups, salmon souffle, stuffings for fish and for fruit cups. It is also used with lamb, veal, beef, ham dishes, duck and rabbit.
SAGE	This is used for pork, sausage, poultry dressing and tomato dishes.
SESAME SEEDS	Used on cookies, bread and confections.
SPEARMINT LEAVES	These leaves are used to flavor mint julep, iced drinks, chewing gum, jelly, peas, new potatoes, mint sauces, etc.
SUMMER SAVORY	This herb is usually cooked with various foods such as lima beans, dried beans, string beans, peas, veal, pork and poultry dressing.

SPICE OR HERB	USES
TARRAGON	A vinegar known as Tarragon Vinegar is made from this herb. It has a flavor very suitable for sauces and for pickling. It is also used in meat, stews, soups and salads.
THYME	This is used with pork, beef, mutton, game, poultry, stews, soups, dressings, sauces, gravies, pickles, vegetables, etc. As the benefits of thyme would rapidly diminish if thyme were to be cooked with the food, the spice should not be placed with the food until about an hour before the cooking is finished.
TUMERIC	The powdered root of the tumeric plant is used in curry powder for a sauce for boiled rice, meats, fish, etc.
VANILLA	This is used for fruit sauces, ice cream, cakes, custards and puddings.

HERB-O-MATIC LOCATOR INDEX

HERBS *(Capital Letters)*
  Or Symptoms, Health Situations,
  Uses, etc.   *Cross Reference*   *Page*

Good Health Begins Right Here

ABC'S OF VITAMINS, MINERALS AND NATURAL FOODS

John Paul Latour

An accurate, up-to-the-minute guide to foods, vitamins, minerals and poisons—their use and abuse. Reveals what to eat and what **not** to eat to achieve radiant good health.   95¢

ENCYCLOPEDIA OF MEDICINAL HERBS

Joseph Kadans, Ph.D.

A practical guide to the medical and cosmetic use of over 600 herbs—with hundreds of simple herbal treatments for all kinds of ailments. Special section on herb and spice cookery.   **$1.50**

LITTLE-KNOWN SECRETS OF HEALTH AND LONG LIFE

Steve Prohaska

How to avoid doctors, dentists, hospitals and medical bills while gaining the blessings of good health and long life through simple, natural means. Features the fabulous Saturation Diet and a proven exercise program.   **$5.95**

THE ARTHRITIS HANDBOOK

Darrell Crain, M.D.

An expert, authoritative guide to alleviating the suffering of arthritis, rheumatism and gout through natural diet and exercise. "A valuable manual."— The Arthritis Foundation   **$1.45**

WINE AND BEER MAKING SIMPLIFIED

H.E. Bravery

The thinking man's handbook—a lucid and lively guide for the home winemaker who knows "what to do" but wants to know "why it works." With a section of recipes from apricot wine to light mild ale.   95¢

HEALTH AND VIGOR AFTER 40 WITH NATURAL FOODS AND VITAMINS

Herman Saussele, D.C.

A practicing chiropractic doctor reveals how men and women in the middle years can start the powerful healing forces of nature working for better health, longer life and more joyful living.   **$1.45**

HEALTH TONIC, ELIXIRS AND POTIONS FOR THE LOOK AND FEEL OF YOUTH

Carlson Wade

Scores of easy-to-make, easy-to-use tonics, potions, and elixirs said to bring relief from seemingly hopeless aches and pains and which may help you look and feel years younger than your actual age.   **$1.45**

HEALTHIER JEWISH COOKERY
The Unsaturated Fat Way

June Roth

Hundreds of traditional Jewish recipes, streamlined to remove the saturated fats and retain the old-fashioned tastes. Substitutes vegetable for animal fat, eliminates frying, uses herbs and natural foods.   **$4.95**

THESE TWO BOOKS
COULD CHANGE YOUR LIFE

NEW HOPE FOR INCURABLE DISEASES

E. Cheraskin, M.D. and
W.M. Ringsdorf, Jr., M.D.

The revolutionary bestseller that proves in simple, everyday language that the battle against many dread diseases previously considered hopeless is being won—today. Stressing simple organic improvements in diet and nutrition and recent dramatic discoveries in these areas, the authors outline radically new and hopeful treatments for some of the most feared ailments of our time—multiple sclerosis, glaucoma, heart disease, mental retardation, birth defects and others. **"It is likely to become the most valuable guide to good health anyone could posess . . . an historic book, a must for all health seekers. The material on food supplements alone, is worth the price of the book."** — Better Nutrition $1.65

REVITALIZE YOUR BODY WITH NATURE'S SECRETS

Edwin Flatto, N.D., D.O.

A respected homeopathic physician explores every aspect of physical and mental well-being, never losing sight of the fact that health is the natural state of the body while disease is an unnatural state of imbalance. Fasting as a way to cleanse the body of toxic waste, the importance of a diet of wholesome, natural foods and the rewards of right eating are covered, as are exercise as therapy and the health benefits of fresh air and sunshine. Scores of questions on the problems of overweight, ulcers, varicose veins, acne, sinus trouble, constipation, colds and other common ailments are answered. Soundly scientific, easy-to-follow, this simple book promises lasting health, undreamed vigor and the happiness and peace that go with them.
$1.45

BLUEPRINTS FOR BETTER HEALTH

VITAMIN E— THE MIRACLE WORKER

Ruth Winter

A simple, scientifically sound and comprehensive book that presents all the facts regarding the superb properties and marvelous potential of Vitamin E. Ruth Winter, a respected medical writer, examines the many claims and counter claims made for this extraordinary vitamin and reveals its reported usefullness in fighting infertility, ulcers and arthritis, its importance in preventing blood clots, its effectiveness against heart disease, cancer in animals and its significant role in retarding the aging process. Essential reading for everyone concerned about their own health and the health of their loved ones. **95¢**

THE FOUNTAIN OF YOUTH

C.E. Burtis

A thorough guide to renewed vigor and well-being through wholesome organically grown foods, combined with a startling, fully documented expose of the adulterants and destructive processing that poison much of our daily fare. Based on a lifetime of research and experimentation in the field of nutrition, Mr. Burtis' book shows exactly how wholesome natural foods can bring renewed youth, vitality, fitness and the priceless gift of a longer life. Here are menus of easy-to-prepare health foods and eating methods that assure the best digestion and fullest use of a food's nourishing qualities as well as a discussion of dangerous foods. **$1.45**

HEALTH and MEDICINE BOOKS

All books are available at your bookseller or directly from ARCO PUBLISHING COMPANY INC., 219 Park Avenue South, New York, N.Y. 10003. Send price of books plus 25¢ for postage and handling. No C.O.D.